The Brand Strategist's Guide to Desire

The Brand Strategist's Guide to Desire

How to give consumers what they actually want

Anna Simpson

First published 2014 by
PALGRAVE MACMILLAN

Palgrave Macmillan in the UK is an imprint of Macmillan Publishers Limited, registered in England, company number 785998, of Houndmills, Basingstoke, Hampshire RG21 6XS.

Palgrave Macmillan in the US is a division of St Martin's Press LLC, 175 Fifth Avenue, New York, NY 10010.

Palgrave Macmillan is the global academic imprint of the above companies and has companies and representatives throughout the world.

Palgrave® and Macmillan® are registered trademarks in the United States, the United Kingdom, Europe and other countries.

ISBN 978–1–137–35181–4

This book is printed on paper suitable for recycling and made from fully managed and sustained forest sources. Logging, pulping and manufacturing processes are expected to conform to the environmental regulations of the country of origin.

A catalogue record for this book is available from the British Library.

A catalog record for this book is available from the Library of Congress.

Typeset by MPS Limited, Chennai, India.

To my sister Ruth, who loves to help others find what they are looking for.

Contents

Foreword

"Brands are the problem!" "Brands are the solution!" So goes a common debate.

The problem with brands, say many, is that they have fuelled an era of over-consumption, which has led to a society groaning at the seams with social inequalities, and a world running perilously low on natural resources.

And the solution camp?

The starting premise for brands as a possible solution to some urgent social, environmental and economic challenges, both locally and globally, requires an evolution of the traditional notion of a brand. They shift from an exclusive focus on transactions. They are no longer just the conduit between a business and the end consumer. They become agents of change.

A new role for brands could be described as naïve optimism. But while trust in government and business is probably at an all-time low, there is at least some trust in brands. In this light, a new role for them becomes easier to envisage.

Brands are more than iconic images splashed across the world's bill boards. They are the window to the business model. In the past, the distance between the business model and the brand was quite a long and often complicated one: the business model was the mechanism to generate maximum growth and profitability, the brand(s) the route to market.

Today, increasing numbers of businesses understand that their ability to create shareholder value, as described by the age-old metrics of growth and profitability, is inextricably linked to how well they can secure access to dwindling resources, how well they treat their staff, how well they know where and how their stuff is made, and how well they can articulate their role in society. In other words, the ability to be commercially successful increasingly depends on the response of a business to an array of macro-environmental and social trends.

And so emerges a new business model. One that is commercially successful, but perhaps not measured purely in terms of growth. One that delivers goods and services that have a social value. And one that operates within one planet's worth of resources. Within this construct of a sustainable business model, the brand shifts from being an adjunct to being the delivery mechanism for the business's purpose. It is the showcase through which the world can see what the business exists to do and how.

Let's think about purpose for a minute. The sustainable brand operates through conversation, collaboration and co-creation. These are the three cornerstones – the 3Cs – of a service-based mechanism. They enable the brand to consider and deliver what we need, rather than making and marketing products regardless.

Our current model of consumerism is flawed. Once basic needs such as hunger and wellness have been met, buying more and more doesn't make us any happier.

Brands with purpose can fuel a transition to sustainable business models. They could indeed be part of the solution to all sorts of problems: social, environmental and economic.

Key to unlocking their purpose is desire. What do the people who are prepared to place trust in them really want from them? Which aspects of their lives will they trust brands with? What is it they really want?

This guide explores that connection, and offers desire as a route to create change.

All brand managers should read and take note.

Sally Uren,
Chief Executive, Forum for the Future

Preface

Desire moves us. It moves us towards each other and towards our goals. It causes us to reach out for things that stimulate our senses and engage our minds.

We walk up a hill to let our eyes dance on the horizon. We cross a street to let our skin feel the sun. We read, converse and travel to entertain our imagination and expand our knowledge.

The energy we all have to enhance our lives can, like any other form of energy, be harnessed – and its value can turn a profit. This profit can be made without compromising the goal, which is quality of life.

People will find value in products and services that bring them closer to the things they really want, and will readily pay for them. Not just once, but again and again.

Which is why a better understanding of desire is an economic opportunity, and one from which brands, in particular, could benefit. People get to know brands, and develop trust in them, just as they do in their peers. If a brand helps them to connect with something they feel enhances their lives, they will recognize its potential to do so again.

As Sally Uren, Chief Executive of the global non-profit Forum for the Future, says, "Brands can do anything that you want them to do: they're astonishing. They can make you want to buy something you never knew you needed. They can make you feel much better about yourself. And, in a world where people don't trust governments and business, and trust their family and peers above all, brands sit somewhere in the middle. They have enormous potential."

It follows that the first step for a brand is to understand what the people they want to bond with desire. If they can help them to find it, they will become trusted allies.

A.S.

Acknowledgements

I am most grateful to all those who took the time to share their valuable insights with me, helping to shape the ideas in this book. In particular, I thank:

Gemma Adams, Rachel Armstrong, Ramon Arratia, Amjad Aslam, David Bent, Phillida Cheetham, Ian Cheshire, Ian Christie, David Edwards, Kathleen Enright, Gunjan Gupta, Peggy Liu, Dax Lovegrove, Adam Lowry, Ben Maxwell, Alan Marks, Marc Mathieu, Atsuko Nakano, Diana Verde Nieto, Ed Paget, Jonathon Porritt, Chris Sherwin, Vincent Stanley, Catarina Tagmark, Sam Thompson, Jody Turner, Laura Underwood and Sally Uren.

I also wish to thank Duncan Jefferies for reading and editing my manuscript with such careful consideration.

Thanks to all my colleagues at Forum for the Future for challenging me over the years. I am also grateful to Judith Kerr, Dr Clare Connors, Dr Laleh Khalili and Martin Wright for their tuition and encouragement. Thank you Deborah, Bob, Jennifer and Tim for providing quiet places to write.

With much love I thank my family and friends for their support, which made all the difference: Mum, who gave me the love of books, Dad, who gave me a dictionary, Ruth, Toby, my housemate Julia, my three fantastic uncles – Brian, Desmond and Norman – and also Aimee, Ania, Ashlee, Chloë, Claire, Clemence, Nikki and Shivani.

Introduction
A guide to desire

This is a guide to help brand strategists consider what people really want in order to enhance their lives, and to think about the role of their brand in responding to these desires. It offers a new framework for understanding desire, based on some of the things that are really important to us: our family, friends and community; the desire to explore, learn and grow; how we experience the world through our senses; our appetite to live life to the full; and what we set out to achieve.

Why is this guide aimed at brand strategists in particular? Because they are the link between a commercial proposition and the lives it means to touch. They can talk to the people the company wants to reach and – more importantly – listen to them. They can start conversations that lead to new ideas for research and development. And they nurture a space for collaboration between the company's operations and its wider context.

Why do brand strategists need a smarter approach to desire? Because consumerism in its current "shop until you drop" form rarely offers real satisfaction, and is facing a crisis: witness the failure of high-street chains such as music retailer HMV in the UK and clothing company American Apparel in the US.[1] At the same time, collaborative consumption is moving from the niche to the mainstream, facilitated by online rental platforms from Airbnb to Zipcar. This creates an opportunity, and an incentive, to do things differently. Other pressures are also pushing companies to innovate – from constraints on key resources, such as water, commodities and land, to the disruption of established markets from innovative entrepreneurs. Think of the challenge to the music industry presented by the likes of YouTube and Spotify. The best way to avoid getting caught out is a clear understanding of what your audience wants, and how your company can offer it.

This guide will help brands get closer to what people desire, and rethink how it can help them to find it. A brand that both enhances people's lives and nurtures the resources on which they depend will prove more resilient, win trust and achieve better results.

A brief note on need and desire

It is impossible to talk about desire without touching on Abraham Maslow, whose theory of a hierarchy of needs (beginning with physiological needs such as food and shelter, and moving 'up' through the needs for security and society towards self-actualization) has influenced many sociologists, economists, marketers and philosophers.[2] Personally, I find such a hierarchy unconvincing in a maze of contrasting motivations – from social expectations, culture and politics, to the availability of resources and simply personal preference. "Need" is a word with gravitas: it seems to imply a compulsion related to survival. "Desire" could be taken to imply indulgence, but also suggests greater agency through the strength of mind to identify and pursue a goal. But both words mask a more complex truth. The apparent need to eat can be overridden by the desire to make a strong statement – to oneself or to others – through starvation. The impression of hunger can be awakened by the sensory pleasure of the scent of bread or bacon. Sleep can be overridden by the desire to stay up late with loved ones or finish watching a film. Similarly, the need to exercise can lose out to the desire to have a nap. As Oscar Wilde quipped, "Whenever I feel like exercise, I lie down until the feeling passes."[3]

My interest is in the distance between where people are and where they would like to be, and the resulting impulse to go and find something that lessens the gap. I talk about desire, rather than need, and use this word to encapsulate the momentum to change ourselves or our circumstances.

Desire for what?

The verb "to desire" comes from the Latin phrase "*de sidere*", which means "from the stars". If you've ever tipped your head back, looked to the skies and wished, you won't find this etymology surprising.

But few people today, including many of faith, expect their desires to be satisfied through celestial good will. We don't just sit back and say, come what may. Instead, we go looking for ways to enhance our lives – whether we set off on the high seas or down the high street.

However, the feeling of desire rarely comes with an answer. People can feel compelled to move, but not know where to go, or what they are looking for. This can leave them highly suggestible. They might sit down in a restaurant feeling hungry, but happy to let their choice be prompted by the menu. They might spend hours browsing shops in the hope of finding the right outfit for a particular occasion. Perhaps what they actually desire, more than a new suit or accessory, is to knock at the door and be greeted by smiles.

The shops are full of objects that seem to promise satisfaction. Many disappoint. What began with the efficiency gains of mass manufacture has become a culture in which we pay little attention to whether what we buy meets the need. Companies market food that's not nutritious, clothes that don't last, birthday cards that replace personal greetings, and travel packages that insulate tourists from foreign culture. It's rare that one size fits all, but millions of labels will try to convince you that it should.

The Chilean economist Manfred Max-Neef discusses the extent to which we find satisfaction in objects and experiences. Some things promise more satisfaction than they actually give, and Max-Neef offers a scale to demonstrate the various ways in which our expectations are either disappointed or exceeded. At the bottom of his scale there are "pseudo-satisfiers": things that don't meet the need, and can even get in the way of satisfaction. For instance, if the need is social status, there's the fancy watch or car that may seem to represent it but won't bring you the genuine respect earned through positive contributions to society. Higher up Max-Neef's scale there are things that do satisfy a need, in the way that food satisfies hunger. At the top are things that satisfy multiple needs – for instance, food that doesn't just abate hunger but enables someone to eat in a way that enhances many aspects of their life. A tasty, nutritious meal enjoyed with family and friends, for example, brings sensory pleasure, health, a sense of community and even cultural rituals – from a clink of glasses and a toast, to blessings, songs and tea ceremonies.[4]

Is satisfaction all it's cracked up to be?

Desire is a renewable source of human energy. A desire met once is by no means a desire fulfilled. As the behavioral economist Daniel Kahneman observes, while the memory of satisfaction may be long-lived, the experience of it is momentary.[5] One response to this is to try and ignore our feelings of desire, to rise above them: this is what Buddhists seek to do, and what the philosopher Arthur Schopenhauer advocated, seeing desire, or the human will, as the root of all suffering. This is rather an extreme stance, considering the many beautiful things people achieve through will and desire, from preparing a delicious dessert to producing a work of art. The fact that they risk disappointment if it doesn't turn out how they wish, or that they may feel the urge to bake another cake that will be even better, seems little reason to give up. As another philosopher, Adam Phillips, observes, we are always going to want something else, and so perhaps we need simply to recognize that "satisfaction is not the answer to life, so to speak. Partly because there isn't an answer to life, but partly because satisfaction isn't always the point."[6]

Phillips proposes that we should value frustration above satisfaction. This may not sound much good as a brand strategy: you don't want to annoy people by keeping the object of temptation beyond their reach. But there is a useful tip here for brands. If the search for satisfaction can be just as valuable to the individual as the goods or service they find, then brands can provide value simply by accompanying them on the quest. Usually, brands focus on products and services that offer satisfaction (to varying extents); they may forget to ask what it is their audience really wants. They miss out on the thrill of the chase.

Another advocate of the quest to better understand what drives people, and what it is that attracts them to certain things, is the change strategist Tom Crompton at WWF-UK. Crompton is interested in what people value, and he distinguishes between intrinsic values, including "the value placed on a sense of community, affiliation to friends and family, and self-development", and extrinsic values: ones that "are contingent upon the perceptions of others [and] relate to envy of 'higher' social strata, admiration of material wealth, or power." Crompton sees these as opposed, and makes the case for civil organizations to activate and strengthen our intrinsic values, "for example, by encouraging people to think about the importance of particular things".[7]

Our values can shape what we desire. When people reflect on what they value, they can find it easier to identify the things they would really like to play a greater role in their lives. For instance, if you value equality, you are likely to desire a fairer society. If you value community, you are likely to desire more time to spend with your family and friends. Crompton talks about the importance of identifying and responding to our intrinsic values, and says that influential peers, the media, education, culture and public policy can all play a role in this. He doesn't mention brands, however.

Brands can awaken both our values and our desires. An opportunity awaits them, in shifting their emphasis away from the products they offer, towards their ability to engage with their audience. They have a positive social role to play in helping people identify their desires and guiding them on their journey to realizing them.

A better conversation

The way brands talk to people is changing. While TV and billboard advertising were the primary channels through which a brand could communicate with its audience, the conversation was more of a broadcast than an exchange. Brands began with an answer, saying: "This is what you desire". Smart marketers, led by the influential Harvard Business School professor and former editor of the *Harvard Business Review* Theodore Levitt, recognized that "people don't buy things but buy solutions to problems".[8] Their role was therefore to help the consumer recognize that they had a problem, and one that could only *really* be met by the product or service on offer. In this model, the company begins with their proposition, adds an idea that helps to set it apart, and hey presto, there's the brand. As Charles Revson said of Revlon, "In the factory we make cosmetics. In the store we sell hope."[9]

Now, we're seeing a shift. The next generation of brands begins by engaging its audience in an open conversation. It asks them what they want, what makes them feel good, what they're looking for. As Philip Kotler, Distinguished Professor of International Marketing at the Kellogg School of Management, argues, "Instead of treating people simply as consumers, marketers approach them as whole human beings with minds, hearts and spirits."[10] Kotler calls this trend Marketing 3.0, and describes it as a "values-driven era". He contrasts this new approach to the mainstream of today, which "assumes the view that consumers are passive targets of marketing campaigns".

This turns the whole process of brand development on its head. A brand's identity is formed through the conversations it has with those people it seeks to reach. These exchanges generate the ideas and culture that shape the brand's purpose, and this in turn helps to create the proposition – whether it's a product, service, experience, or all of the above. It's a collaborative, creative journey, on which the brand and its audience set out together.

D – C – B – A

I call this new approach the D – C – B – A of brand strategy.

It begins with a better understanding of desire (D). This understanding helps the company to define its culture and character (C), which others then recognize and associate with it as a brand (B). The brand uses its conversations to co-create actions (A), which respond in meaningful ways to the desire(s) of its audience. It's the reverse of the standard practice I described earlier, the A – B – C – D approach, in which a company begins with its action – creating a product, such as shampoo – upon which it superimposes its brand, and then goes about creating a culture ("beauty is wavy hair with a particular sheen") to incentivize desire for the product ("I must buy this particular shampoo in order to be beautiful").

The danger in sticking with the familiar A – B – C – D formula is that your brand might get all the way to D and find that the desire has shifted. This is the story of the likes of HMV and the camera company Jessops, two brands which failed on the high street when they persistently peddled a product after consumer desire had shifted to digital models.

The problem for these brands was the assumption that people valued the product more than the purpose it served; whereas for the consumers, the most high-tech nifty 35" camera was no more than a means to an end they no longer wanted. Instead of albums thick

Turns the whole process of brand development on its head

with holiday snaps and framed prints, Jessops' audience wanted easy access to photographic memories they could share online, and digital did the trick better. Likewise, the boxed CDs on HMV's shelves proved no match for the tracks easily available on demand via iTunes, YouTube and Spotify.

The rapid scale and success of innovative business models has helped to nurture a culture in which change is expected, prompting people to think afresh about what they want. They realize they no longer need to own so much stuff. They can exchange goods and services with their peers. They can pool their resources, creating large libraries of anything from digital media to garden tools. With the potential to trade their time and skills at will, they feel richer: not only do they have greater buying power, but they have more to contribute. They have a deeper sense of connection to those around them. This sense of empowerment is no counter-force to desire. After years of tightened belts, many people feel it's time life looked up. They're ready to reach out – but towards what? What do they desire?

Companions with purpose

Research suggests that consumers value a sense of companionship with brands; they may even value it more than the product or service they buy. Meaningful interaction is the difference between a brand that people appreciate and one they care nothing about, whether or not the product itself is satisfying. A major survey by the global advertising agency Havas Media, involving over 134,000 consumers across 23 countries, found that most people worldwide would not care if more than 73 per cent of brands disappeared tomorrow.[11] This doesn't imply that brands can't establish relationships the people do care about or would miss. Another survey of consumers in six major international markets, conducted by BBMG, GlobeScan and SustainAbility, found that two-thirds of respondents were "interested in sharing their ideas, opinions and experiences with companies to help them develop better products or create new solutions".[12] This interest in exchange and co-creation, over the mere attraction of existing products, is no bad thing in a world undergoing rapid change. If a brand is defined by its character and the value it adds to a creative process, as opposed to by the products themselves, it will be able to shift its business in more radical ways, and yet keep the social capital which makes it successful.

People don't just want a relationship with a brand for the sake of it, though: they want brands to contribute something meaningful to their lives. "Something meaningful" isn't asking too much. Havas found that people are not looking for "Utopian" lives: they just want "lives that are incrementally better, in meaningful terms. They don't expect any single brand to deliver everything, but they look for specific wellbeing benefits from each brand."

As Kotler explains:

> In a world full of confusion, [consumers] search for companies that address their deepest needs for social, economic, and environmental justice in their mission, vision, and values. They look for not only functional and emotional fulfillment but also human spirit fulfillment in the products and services they choose.

"I am not a consumer"

An anecdote told to me by Ian Cheshire, Chief Executive of the home improvement retail group Kingfisher, offers a good illustration of the desire people feel to be recognized as more than a mere consumer, even when talking to a brand. Cheshire had been speaking to the Forum of Young Global Leaders at the World Economic Forum in Davos, Switzerland, when one of them piped up and (as he put it) told him off. "I am not a consumer", she said. "I hate being described as a consumer. I am a user and a collaborator, and I'm happy to do things in those spaces." Cheshire describes this "abiding memory" as a bit of a turning point in how he thinks and talks about the relationship between people and brands. "Are you a consumer if you are a user of Zipcar [a car-sharing club], for instance?" he asks. "You might be, but that's certainly very different from buying and owning a car and then not using it."

The young leader at DAVOS is not alone: the way in which people think about their role in society is changing. The study led by BBMG found that seven in ten "believe in voting and advocating for issues important to me". But while they recognize their power as consumers, many no longer see this as the first way in which they can influence the world around them. The rise of democratized media and peer-to-peer networks has helped them to find a new currency in words and deeds, bringing a sense of purpose beyond their spending habits, and prompting them to call these habits into question.

Back in 2010, an earlier survey by Havas, which canvassed nearly 6000 people across seven countries, found that 67 per cent believed they would be better off if they lived more simply and 72 per cent were trying to improve how they live. The report concluded: "We are witnessing a broad and fundamental shift away from mindless hyperconsumerism and towards an approach that is at once more conscious and more satisfying."[13] Similarly, the BBMG study, which surveyed over 6000 respondents in Brazil, China, Germany, India, the UK and the US, found that 66 per cent said we need to consume less, and 85 per cent said that friends and family are the most important things in life.[14]

A world of difference

If people no longer wish to be addressed by brands as consumers, what is the alternative? How can brands engage with people in a more holistic way, taking their complex lives into account, and what role should they then play? This is one of the key questions for strategists, and this guide aims to help them answer it.

The more people explore their values and social purpose, the more they will expect the brands they respect to do this too. For a multinational with diverse audiences, responding to this expectation could seem quite a challenge. Residents from countries as distinct as Brazil, Japan, the Netherlands and the US may well respond in similar ways to surveys, but this does not imply that they share the same desires or are subject to the same influences. In each market, particular social, cultural, economic and geographical factors are at play, and these shape the aspirations of their citizens. Any good brand will be aware of the need to recognize these differences in order to have valuable conversations with multiple audiences. The quality of a brand's relationships will depend on its understanding of everything from local etiquette and idioms to the infrastructure for information and communications technology.

As Levitt wrote, "To differentiate an offering effectively requires knowing what drives and attracts customers. It requires knowing how customers differ from one another and how those differences can be clustered into commercially meaningful segments. If you're not thinking segments, you're not thinking."[15]

But in the era of Marketing 3.0, differentiation is no longer enough. It has been superseded by personalization. Thinking in segments won't bring a brand close enough to the desires of its audience. Today, if a brand isn't thinking *people* – and, more importantly, getting to know them – it's not thinking.

Many Chinas, one dream

A pair of contrasting perspectives – one from China, one from Japan – may help to illustrate the importance of local contexts to any meaningful conversation. Peggy Liu is Chairperson of the Shanghai-based Joint US-China Collaboration on Clean Energy (JUCCCE) and the founder of China Dream. She aims to bring together professionals in advertising, storytelling, sustainability and culture, in order to shape a new dream of prosperity for people in China – just as the American Dream has shaped the ideals of US citizens. China's growing middle class may aspire to Western forms of consumerism, but Liu believes a new model is needed – and desired – by Chinese citizens and government: "One that is more suited to Chinese culture and context. One that reimagines prosperity and incorporates sustainability."

China Dream is a new set of social norms that have been built via a co-creation process with a diverse set of influencers. It starts with exploring what it looks like for a middle-class Chinese to thrive in their community. Various intensive dialogues have helped shape the China Dream, such as a health and wellness workshop at Ogilvy China,[16] a culture and style workshop at JinTai Art Museum, and a communities workshop at the Shanghai Tongji University Sino-Finnish Center. For Liu, the key to a powerful China Dream is "curating an inspirational view of personal prosperity", based on values such as "safe food, air and water; vibrant living; moving ahead by building upon our heritage, and convenient and connected communities".[17]

Even though the initiative was born in a very specific cultural context, Liu believes the co-creation process, which aims to redefine consumer aspirations in the light of shared values, can be applied anywhere in the world. Drawing upon the China Dream experience, Liu and colleague Julian Borra of Thin Air Factory have created an open source "Dream-in-a-Box" methodology. A spin-off Dream has also sprung up in the UK Dream, and dialogues have even begun in the US, bringing the search for meaning full circle.

Liu sees an important role for brands in activating the China Dream via marketing campaigns, rather than looking at sustainability through their Corporate Social Responsibility (CSR) initiatives. In China, she says, there is a huge appetite for trustworthy brands that make people feel safe in light of the many food safety issues and pollution problems the country has faced.

> We've had melamine in the milk; we've seen 16,000 pigs floating down the Huangpu River in Shanghai. In China, 90 per cent of water sources are non-drinkable. In rural areas, I'd never buy a bottle of water, because I don't know if they've refilled it and are selling it to me with algae in it. We've seen cardboard in our dumplings instead of meat, lamb that turned out to be fox and mink…

If a brand can use a culture of openness and responsibility to win trust in such a context, it has an immediate advantage with Chinese consumers.

She is looking to luxury brands to revive and refresh Chinese traditions, many of which have been lost through the Cultural Revolution:

> There are thousands of years of Chinese cultural history. There's so much tradition in China that the West doesn't even know about, and that young Chinese citizens can learn from and be proud about. We ask how we can incorporate this history into the luxury brands such as Hermes' new Shang Xia brand.

Liu also sees an opportunity for consumer-facing, mid-market brands, which she believes have an opportunity to win customer loyalty by playing to the aspirational vision of China Dream. "Brands can create a customer community that works with the brand to help achieve together aspects of the China Dream. This means evolving from a functional sale to a much more engaging experiential sale."

For instance, she says, developers such as Lend Lease can work with retailers to create much-needed social spaces in China, moving from ownership of space to access. "Instead of retail centers, they can create lifestyle centers that benefit people who are accustomed to living in small apartments."

A post-Fukushima perspective

Japan is renowned for its luxury consumer markets. The Japan External Trade Organization (JETRO) claims that Japanese consumers are responsible for approximately 30-40 per cent of all global luxury-brand purchases annually. This is no surprise, for now at least: Tokyo has more millionaires than anywhere else in the world.[18] However, a shift away from material aspirations is now underway. Why? Alongside years of deflation and slow growth, JETRO cites the economic and cultural impact of the Fukushima Dai-ichi nuclear disaster, following the Tōhoku earthquake and tsunami in 2011. This incident was not just the result of a coincidence of natural disaster with technological failure, it was the failure of a company to act responsibly: in October 2012, the Tokyo Electric Power Company (Tepco) published a report admitting that it had not put in place sufficient measures to prevent disaster, through fear of being further challenged about the safety of its plants.[19]

The Japanese designer and entrepreneur Atsuko Nakano described to me the impact of this incident on consumer culture:

> We had a very tough period just after this experience of terrible disaster. We started to notice that it is not material things that we want. We want spiritual feelings, love. In my opinion, Japanese people want to experience more on the inside: not luxury in material. They prefer warmth of connecting to each other. It's my opinion. For me, my family and friends are indispensable to my life; feeling connected and being linked with others is very important.[20]

Nakano makes candles that cast the shadow of a flower when they burn, for ritual events celebrating the milestones in family life, such as birth and marriage. She sees her designs as a way to bridge the gap between the invisible life of feelings and the visible, aesthetic realm.

I asked her which came first: the design of the candle or the message of ritual celebration. "The message", she replied, without hesitation. "On this project, the theme is life. I want to send a message of an equal chance of life. I was thinking about the best way to express it, there are so many options. I chose a candle, because it is connected to events about life: birthdays, religious ceremonies. And I chose a flower because it is living. Flowers have a beginning and an end, and they are always transforming. This is about life, not stuff. This candle, as a sign of the powerful presence of the invisible, is appealing because usually we can't see the flower: it appears when you light the candle."

Nakano's candles are her response to a cultural context she has taken care to understand, in which she recognized the desire to feel such a strong bond with those you love that it almost glows. She began with an understanding of desire, and this became the cultural basis on which she built her business. She developed the message, and then the design for an object she would sell. It's the ideal D – C – B – A approach.

Brands as eye-openers

It's no secret – few people know what they want. They may know what they value, but they may not know how to give these things a greater role in their lives. They may love their family and friends, and yet not be able to find more time to spend with them. They may enjoy the taste of home-grown food more than anything they ever find in a restaurant, but not know how to grow vegetables from seed, or have the space to cultivate them. They may feel most useful when a friend in need sends them out on an urgent mission, or when a colleague gives them an important task to master, but may not have recognized the pleasure a sense of purpose can bring. Helping people to join up the dots, by asking the big questions about what really will enhance their lives, is a major opportunity for brands. It's also an opportunity for society. If brands are so bold as to challenge their audience to approach life in new ways, with new aspirations, they can shift behaviors in a direction that might prove better for us all.

It's a massive opportunity for innovation and one pioneers in business are already spotting. As Ian Cheshire observes:

> We [at Kingfisher] have come to the conclusion that most of what consumers are doing is looking for answers from brands and businesses.

The brand has a permanent invitation to come up with new suggestions. I think the right type of brands, those that are authentic, have a lot of scope to challenge consumers to do more, to be more, and to provide something other than a transactional, functional product. I think the opportunity is there; it's then translating it into reality.

For Cheshire, this opportunity is certainly a commercial one, but also one which could strengthen the social and environmental context in which a business operates. He is a pioneer of the "Net Positive" movement, which encourages businesses to contribute, both to society and to the environment, more than they take in time and resources. For him, it's a no-brainer: if you take more than you give, you are pulling out the rug from under your own feet. And how do you expect your employees to feel good about that? Whereas, if you give more than you take, the whole brand benefits from a real sense of purpose, and this will be recognized by the wider world.

The first step towards this is seeing the big picture, and this is something consumers and brands can do together. Alan Marks, Senior Vice President Global Communications at eBay Inc., believes the primary role of a brand is to help its audience gain a better understanding of their surroundings and the opportunities at their feet. He refers to the 1977 film *Powers of Ten*, in which the frame zooms out from a couple on a picnic rug by a lakeside in Chicago, to outer space and back again, enlarging the scene by a power of ten each second.

"It's our job to make sense of it all," says Marks. "It's our responsibility to understand the picnic, to see the neighborhood, to know the shoreline and to intuit the broader environment in which our customers, our employees and our stakeholders exist. That's how we can begin to build belief."[21]

Moving to Action

A quick recap of D – C – B – A. The brand introduces itself, learns the local language, opens a conversation, and takes time to listen to the people it encounters and build a sense of what they are looking for, or what they need, to enhance their lives. Then it looks back at itself, its culture and characteristics, and asks what value it can bring. Next, it looks at how it can make this added value absolutely central to everything it does. And then it's time for action.

At the action stage, brand strategists find themselves in a similar position to designers and product developers. They begin with the same open questions, looking for new approaches to the fabric and infrastructure of daily life, beyond habit and familiarity. A good outcome begins with the people you're designing for. The innovation consulting firm IDEO has developed a model called human-centered design, which looks at any new creation through three lenses: desirability, feasibility and viability. Most importantly, the result should meet the desires of the people it has been designed for, but it is also crucial that it is both technologically and financially viable. Any sensible designer will take a long-term perspective, asking not just whether its proposition is feasible now but whether it will be resilient in years to come. Does it depend on resources that will still be available in the future? Can it be produced in a way that ensures they are?

Brands should ask these questions too, and involve their audience in the same way. The main difference for a brand is that they needn't settle on one solution. They might work with their audience to co-create a whole suite of complementary products and services – but even these shouldn't end the conversation. The more a brand can encourage its audience to keep exploring their desires and asking how best to meet them, the deeper the relationship will grow and the longer it will last. It will also mean the audience is involved at every stage of the brand's own development. The exploration of desire through on-going interaction with the brand becomes its central proposition; the focus is no longer on satisfaction, but on the journey itself. Nor does this have to end in consumption.

It's a similar concept to the mantra of Marshall McLuhan, the Canadian communication theorist credited with predicting the influence of the internet, 30 years before its invention. In his words, "the medium is the message".[22] I argue that engagement *is* the brand proposition. The conversations a brand shares about what people really want, and what it can offer in return, is as important as anything it puts on a shelf.

Three rewards for desire-led brands

If brands can engage in meaningful conversation with people about their desires, and support them to move towards these things, they will reap three rewards.

The first is a stronger identity: one that is both more attractive and more resilient. The brand consultancy Dragon Rouge proposes five elements that make a business "beautiful" in the eyes of the wider world: integrity, which comes from a clear sense of purpose; curiosity, through looking at the world "with originality and optimism"; elegance, which is "not simply a matter of aesthetics" but of empathy with your audience; craft, by approaching design with the skill and care of a human touch; and finally, prosperity, through bold decision-making.[23] The quest better to understand what people desire will help a brand to achieve all five aspects of a beautiful business; indeed, they will be crucial tools on the journey.

The second reward is more meaningful relationships, ones with the potential to grow and develop throughout life and even be handed on to the next generation. Brands that use multiple channels to listen, engage and interact will be met with loyalty and recommendations, especially as the "like, share and advise" culture of sites like Facebook and TripAdvisor grows. According to IBM's 2013 report "The State of Marketing", leading companies are over five times more likely to adopt cross channel technologies in engaging with their customers. It also notes that "$83 billion is lost each year in the US from poor customer experiences".[24] Another report into the value of customer service, by the Nielsen and McKinsey joint venture NM Incite, found that 71 per cent of people are likely to recommend a brand which listens to their "questions, issues, needs and concerns, and address[es] them".[25]

The third reward is a catalyst for innovation. The two central questions in this guide – "What do people desire?" and "How can my brand help them reach it?" – will revive a brand's sense of purpose and prompt it to imagine new ways of achieving its mission. As Forum for the Future's CEO Sally Uren says, "The brands that are doing really well at the moment are the ones which are going to consumers and saying, 'Hey, what would you like?' or 'We've got this issue, help us solve it!' or 'Talk to us about whether or not you like that product and if you didn't, what should we do differently?'" She mentions MyStarbucksIdea.com, a crowd-sourcing initiative which used social media to encourage Starbucks customers to say what they'd like to change. If Starbucks got above 10,000 "asks" for the same development, it would take it to the board for permission to go ahead with it. Winning ideas range from LED lighting to the option to pay for your coffee with your mobile phone, to new recipes for cookies. Uren believes this sort of consumer-led open innovation is the way forward: "It's really clever. From a business point of view, it means any new ideas you put out there, you've already tested them."

Five perspectives on desire

This guide offers five perspectives on desire. These are not the only ways of thinking about desire: there are many more. They are merely five useful starting points that I have identified and wished to explore. Their order here has a certain poetry for me, but it does not imply a hierarchy.

We begin with *community*: the desire to be among other people and relate to them. We move on through *adventure*, the desire to explore and to grow; *aesthetics*, the desire to experience the world around us through our senses; and *vitality*, the desire to live life to the full. Finally, we come to our end, or *purpose*: the desire to give life meaning.

Each chapter considers how desire for this particular aspect of life is manifest in different societies and cultures. It asks what global and local trends are currently affecting the ability of people to respond to this desire, and to create the right place for it in their lives. And, most importantly, it asks what roles a brand can play.

chapter 1

Community

The desire to be among other people is manifest throughout human history. There are, of course, cases of sought-after solitude: Sybil in her cave, Jesus in the desert, Siddhartha by the tree. Yet these celebrated figures used their time apart to develop insights which later helped them perform revered social roles, as a seer, prophet or teacher. Even the introverts among us come together in shared solitude, quietly appreciating the presence of others in libraries or centers for retreat.

Community defines many aspects of society the world over. We celebrate our connections to each other through cultural rituals, often sharing food or drink with symbolic associations. We read stories or sing songs to reinforce shared understandings of our history and the values we share as a society. Narrative and representational art has played a role in community culture for as many as 40,000 years, and perhaps more. A recent exhibition at the British Museum displayed sculptural representations and engravings of people and animals that have endured since the last Ice Age.[1]

During the Islamic month of Ramadan, Muslims come together at sunset to break their fast together by observing *Iftar*, a shared meal often comprising dates; these emulate the way in which the Prophet Muhammad ended his own fast. At Epiphany, French Catholic families share the *Galette des Rois*, a cake in which a small porcelain figure, the *feve*, is hidden; whoever finds it is named the king of the feast, recalling the search of the magi for the new-born child. In Japan, the cultural concept *ichi-go ichi-e* – that each meeting should be treasured as it may not happen again – is expressed through the Way of Tea, a ceremony which can last up to four hours, depending on the season, the degree of formality and the number of guests.

With such strong traditions and varied practices to celebrate the role of community in our lives, what can brands bring to the feast? Skeptics of the positive role businesses can play in society may respond to such a question with cynicism. But why should it be a bad thing for brands to offer people something they can really value, as opposed to a seemingly endless supply of disposables and *in*valuables? There's money to be made, of course. Think of the considerable sums people pay to be a member of a club, where they can find people with similar socio-cultural anchors.

The assumption of skeptics is that if you pay to be part of a community, then your experience of it will be less authentic and less satisfactory. This isn't necessarily the case. The money spent is for the context and time in which the relationships can be enjoyed, as opposed to the social bonds themselves. All relationships and communities require some infrastructure: a space to meet (be it physical or virtual), activities to pursue, and ways to recognize each other – from a scout's uniform to a football club scarf.

The important thing is that a brand proposition adds value. To enhance the role of community in people's lives, a brand needs to ask them what it is they are looking for, and in what respects they might appreciate a helping hand. The following four sections offer some prompts, by focusing on some elements of community that attract people: belonging, exchange and identity.

Belonging, not just belongings

People like to belong, and theories abound as to why. Many take natural selection as a starting point, emphasizing our competitive nature, driven by the need to survive, find food and attract a mate. Marketers have made this a self-fulfilling prophecy, appealing to status – and particularly sexual status – in order to market their wares, from deodorant to cars to shoes. The products certainly sell, but whether they actually make us more attractive, or even help us to feel more attractive, is debatable. Do they help us to feel we belong? Perhaps, as the child compares his toys with others in the playground, or the freelancer exchanges a nod with another tablet-user in the café. But is this really what we are looking for when we feel left out?

It's not just belongings that are sold on the basis of status. Marketers also appeal to status when they want to sell the sense of belonging, through VIP packages to "exclusive" clubs, or hard-to-win entry to member-based organizations. The belief that status drives much of our behavior is common among business strategists and philosophers alike. The French philosopher René Girard argued that the desire a person experiences for an object is always influenced by a third party.[2] They feel this desire, Girard argues, because they hold another person who possesses it in esteem; the object becomes a symbol of that esteem. For example, your desire for a particular perfume comes from an association of that perfume with someone you esteem: perhaps someone who wears it, or the brand itself. Girard's theory dates from 1961, but over 50 years later, similar arguments still carry weight. Communications expert Solitaire Townsend, co-founder of the consultancy Futerra, makes status the heart of her thesis in a recent paper, "The Naked Environmentalist". She writes: "The fight for status, the desire to look desirable, and wanting to be well thought of are the secret motivations which drive a great deal of our behavior, as well as taking up a great deal of our daily mental attention."[3]

The contemporary essayist Alain de Botton takes the role that others play in determining what we desire a step further. He argues that, in contemporary Western culture, we are only able to appreciate our own wellbeing through comparing it to that of other people and finding ourselves better off. It's a rather depressing perspective.

Whatever the extent to which the desire for status drives our actions, it is possible that we latch on to it mistakenly. We may seek out exclusivity and popularity when what we really want is social interaction. Ramon Arratia, Sustainability Director at the global carpet tile company Interface, described to me very eloquently what he values in relationships:

> When you speak, people listen to you; people call you to ask you for things, which shows you that they value your opinion. It's about quality of relationships – not just quantity. At the moment, we have a society where things move so fast and people know so little about you that they just look at you for a second. They look at your clothes and then at your

business card. We need to move into a place where you aren't just your looks and your job title.[4]

Nonetheless, Arratia is doubtful that the desire for status will ever become less attractive. The way forward, he argues, is towards more meaningful ways of attracting the interest of others – for instance, through developing skills in sport, becoming an amateur historian, or playing an instrument. These are extremely expensive ways to set yourself apart, he concedes: hence the business case for promoting them.

For Townsend, the fundamental driver behind all of this is sex, with procreation as the aim. Like Arratia, she believes that the desire for social status needs to be met, and that it could be done more effectively through a new model. She argues that status could be completely dissociated from wealth, through "an entirely new, totally transformative mechanism by which human beings compete, sexually display and build status virtually, rather than through material consumption." This, she argues, could lead to radical dematerialization of the economy. Signs of virtual status symbols are already emerging: people pride themselves on their extensive Twitter following, and even earn money for tweets, or enjoy perks accorded by social influence rating agencies like Klout.

But is status really all that important to us? In my experience, few people would say they desire it, even if they are happy to admit that it sometimes influences some choice or other. Arguably, it is an assumption that social status is somehow "worth it" that has driven many Western societies to prize economic growth *per capita* above wellbeing *per community*. The results aren't impressive. The new economic foundation's Happy Planet Index – which measures the reported wellbeing of populations across over 150 nations – found that nine out of the ten top-ranking countries were not in the neoliberal West, but in Latin America and the Caribbean, with Costa Rica taking the first place two years in a row.[5]

There is an irony in the understanding that we will pay a high price to belong to a community, only in order to set ourselves apart from other people. A promising counter-theory comes not from any denial of evolutionary theory, but from a new interpretation of it, in which collaboration plays as great a role as competition. David Sloan Wilson, Distinguished Professor for Biological Sciences and Anthropology at Binghamton University, New York, talks about a new "science of cooperation" which is emerging as a result of new research by evolutionary biologists. It's a mistake, Sloan

Wilson explains, to consider that society can function on the basis of competition alone: we also need to collaborate: "One thing that's very encouraging for people in cooperative movements is that small face-to-face groups have emerged as a natural human unit. We have developed a set of instincts, which we think of as our moral psychology, and which cause us to function very well in small groups".[6] A new understanding of our desire for belonging, based not on difference and competition but on mutual appreciation and companionship, could inspire new behaviors – and new roles for brands. Richard Sennett, the renowned Professor of Social Science at LSE and MIT, argues that cooperation is one of the key skills we need to sustain everyday life. It "oils the machinery of getting things done", he says, adding that the process of understanding and responding to each other is a "thorny" one, "full of difficulty and ambiguity". Ritual, he explains, is one of the ways in which society has sought to balance competition and cooperation, giving a structure to social exchange.[7] Brands can shape social rituals: they can set the rules in defined contexts, and make certain behaviors more acceptable than others. They could do more, nurturing collaboration and offering new contexts in which cooperation is both expected and rewarded. As Sloan Wilson comments:

> If you have a certain set of ideas that causes you to see the world a certain way, then this governs how you behave. Our current narrative emphasizes individual self-interest. If we can adopt a different narrative, then all of a sudden there'll be new possibilities, new solutions that we can trial. Let's think about what could actually improve our quality of life. Let's implement it.[8]

Health professionals and social policy makers are already developing new strategies based on evidence that the sense of belonging enhances mental wellbeing.[9] It's time for brands to take the lead.

CHALLENGE YOUR BRAND

- Do you offer a sense of status, or a sense of belonging?
- What can you learn from other community hubs, such as sports leagues and youth centers?
- How could you promote cooperation between small groups of people?

Exchange, not just trade

Wander through the terraces of any sunny street, pop into any beauty salon, scroll through any online forum: it's hard to deny the pleasure people get from exchanging their ideas and perceptions. It doesn't take long for this pleasure to become associated with the places in which they experience it. This is because exchange depends on trust: we need a safe space to develop the confidence to offer our opinions or skills or belongings to other people, knowing how they will be received, and what we can expect in return.

As Nancy Lowery, President of the Hayden Chamber of Commerce in North Idaho, writes:

> Some of my fondest memories include the shops and restaurants that I visited often [in the area in which I grew up]. There was a safety in shopping and eating in places where they knew me and looked out for me. I developed a strong connection with my hometown, in part because of this. To this day there is a Facebook page for those who grew up in that area where routinely members are posting things like "Do you remember the little corner candy shop" or "Is the Lamplighter Restaurant still around?"[10]

When Lowery joined the board of the Hayden Chamber, her goal was to build and strengthen business in and around Hayden. She discovered that she had something "incredibly powerful" to tap into: community. Economies depend on strong associations. It is through trust that economies thrive, developing shared concepts of value that form the foundation for the exchange of all sorts of commodities: time against wages, wages against food, food against services, services against hospitality, and so on. Brands are the safeguards of trust in these economies. Their reputation can not only be used to build to their own business, but to offer a foundation for all sorts of exchange.

As Lowery observes:

> The very idea of community comes into being because people like to cooperate with each other. We share our work and this ... leads to our dependency on other people working in different roles. For example, the

cobbler repairs shoes for us, the barber cuts our hair, the tailor stitches fashionable clothes for us, the butcher cuts meat for us, the baker prepares biscuits for us, engineers make houses for us, etc. All these individuals fall into a community, without whom our lives would be very difficult.

Lowery's insights are drawn from her experience of a community formed on the basis of a shared location. The rise of online platforms means a similar sort of exchange now occurs between people who have never met or even spoken to each other in real time, who live on different continents, and even in communities with little shared understanding. If trust and reputation are the basis for exchange, it would seem unlikely that local economies could be transferred to a virtual realm. And yet eBay is just one of many brands facilitating exchange between people who have nothing in common other than the services they can render each other. I asked Alan Marks, Senior Vice President Global Communications at eBay Inc., about the value of community to commerce.

> If you think back to the founding of eBay in 1995, the idea that total strangers anywhere in the world could come together and trade what they have was pretty crazy to a lot of people. But Pierre Omidyar [the founder of eBay] believes deeply in trusting people, and that if you give people the right tools, people will do great things. Ordinary people can use this platform to pursue their passion, create a livelihood for themselves, give back to the community, create new models of consumption, new entrepreneurial models, new retail models. We think that's very powerful.

It may not feel like a great act of trust to expect an eBay seller to pop an item in the post, with all the assurance of the feedback of their former customers. But that's because eBay has provided a context in which the reputation of each individual matters, thereby creating a safe space in which such trust is possible, not unlike Lowery's Lamplighter Restaurant.

As people develop more collaborative relationships with brands, moving from the role of consumer towards co-creator, it will shift the way in which safe spaces are developed. Think of the example set by MyStarbucks, which we discussed in the Intro-duction. People want to be involved in the design of their environments, as this space will shape their behaviors: whether they sit, stand or walk; talk loudly or read quietly; mingle with strangers or stick to friends. Professor Rachel Armstrong of Greenwich University, a world expert in biotechnology, leads research into "design fiction", the process of involving people in creating visions of new environments, and exploring how these contexts could shape the way they live their lives. In her words, "The space of possibility is always greater than the event": so, the more we can be stimulated by the world around us and feel free from constraint, the greater the potential for creativity and exchange of ideas.

Armstrong points to the industrial- and technological-solutions provider IBM as a leader in co-creation. Its Smarter Cities project doesn't set out to build cities, but to develop visions for them alongside other organizations who can contribute resources. IBM offers a space for creative interaction, through mass online brainstorms, blogging platforms and live discussions. For instance, a group of six IBM professionals spent three weeks in Málaga, Spain, working closely with the local government and corporate stakeholders – such as the General Director of the Andalucia Technology Park and the founder of Arpa Solutions, a small business specializing in smartphone applications and games. They discussed problems such as high youth unemployment and identified the need to encourage a new culture of entrepreneurship among residents suffering from the loss of thousands of government-funded jobs. These conversations convinced the Mayor, Francisco de la Torre, that the city needs a rebrand to attract more start-up companies who will drive its technological development, thereby creating more jobs.[11] And ultimately, more work for IBM itself.

CHALLENGE YOUR BRAND

- Where do your peers feel most comfortable?
- How can you help to create a safe space for exchange?
- What will people remember about your brand in years to come?

Identity, not just image

Many purchases are motivated by concern for our image. Psychoanalysts argue that our very sense of self is formed through the realization that other people are looking, a concept developed by the influential French theorist Jacques Lacan. He spoke of the mirror stage: the point at which an infant first sees its reflection, and so develops an awareness of itself as someone whom other people can see from the outside, just as the child perceives other people.[12] The American philosopher Judith Butler observes a similar phenomenon in conversation: she argues that it is when someone calls out to us, or addresses us, that we recognize ourselves. They say, "Hey you!", and we turn around and say, "Who, me?" – and this exchange confirms that we really do exist in their world, too, and therefore in our own. Butler goes on to explain how this exchange affects our sense of responsibility towards other people. Our identity is built on the assumption that we will behave as they expect us to: we will turn round and answer when they call. By rising to this we build confidence in ourselves.

When we say we "identify" with someone else, this is what we mean: that we recognize their sense of self and so reinforce our own. In a similar way, people also identify with brands. They develop relationships with brands in which they recognize elements of themselves, or which reflect an image of themselves that they aspire towards.

Marc Mathieu, Senior Vice President of Marketing at Unilever, observes this identity–creation in the way people relate to all sorts of brands in their lives, and this can include their country and religion. For brand America, he says, the image is liberty and the pursuit of happiness.

> When you go round the world, you have access because you're an American. I know that image is a little bit less shiny than it may have been in the past, but in the end you have the American dream: you are able to go from where you are today to a place that is likely to be better in years to come.

Mathieu's admittedly broad definition of brands is based on a sense of give-and-take, or mutual responsibility:

> It's the combination of a transaction and an idea. The questions are: what exchange do you have with the brand, and then what benefit do you get from the brand? In terms of America, there's a very clear transaction. I happen to be a US resident and I was on the beach in Los Angeles, and there were some great life guards on the beach and on boats, making

sure the surfers don't have accidents. My wife said, "They're really doing a great job", and I said, "Yes, we're paying for it!" That's the transaction that exists between brand America and the citizens.[13]

So, the identity of an American citizen depends on this exchange: the tax they pay in return for security and infrastructure. Their desire to buy into this "social contract" depends on America's image and the sense of self they will gain through association with it.[14]

Over the course of the 20th century, and particularly since the birth of the internet, the media has played an increasing role in the way in which we perceive ourselves. People don't just look in the mirror, but at images of themselves in photos and films, shared on Facebook and YouTube. As a result, some critics argue, our behavior has begun to change. How we are perceived and how we will be remembered takes on such importance that we behave in ways that will enhance the film or the photo, sometimes we even do this at the expense of the moment itself: we smile for the camera but forget to smile for our companions.

The philosopher of technology and culture D. E. Wittkower points out that few of us actually cook elaborate meals for each other, or get together to sing and perform, compared to the millions of viewers drawn by TV shows such as *Masterchef*, *American Idol* and *Britain's Got Talent*. He observes that:

> [W]hen we do actually cook or sing for others, we do so with these spectacles of cooking or singing before us as models. The meal becomes about the boned duck or the unbroken hollandaise – it is not, as it should be, about spending time together. Singing becomes about performance and fame and glamor and stardom, not about the feeling of your body resonating along with another.[15]

This mediatized perception of ourselves is often blamed for a rise in anxiety and related health problems, such as eating disorders.[16] The danger is that we focus too much on how we are perceived, and not enough on the enjoyment we actually get from spending time with others. We become passive observers of our own lives, rather than living in the moment.

Can we move away from a society in which we mimic the media towards more authentic ways of spending time together? Some leading brands are already looking for ways to help people achieve a stronger sense of identity by focusing on their relationships as opposed to their image. Ian Cheshire, CEO of Kingfisher Group, described how the board of B&Q is using social media to find ways to do this:

> We get the board of B&Q talking about our concept of "better homes, better lives": what it means to them, and the emotional impact of their home-life. We've done a lot of storytelling: retweeting or sharing on Facebook stories to embed people's experiences in our culture. If you get people actually talking about what it means to them to have their brothers and sisters and everyone sit round a table together, in a way they thought they'd never be able to afford, then [as an employee of B&Q] you say "You played a role in that", instead of "You sold another three units of a kitchen".

All brands could benefit from this process, says Cheshire. "The first step is actually knowing what your customers are doing and why. The second is trying to improve their experience." For a house of brands like Kingfisher, which owns various DIY retailers across the world, understanding its customers and improving their experience means keeping a very open mind to cultural differences and expectations. A concept like "home" is by no means universal: there's no parallel word in French, but the phrase "chez soi" (literally, "at one's own") is used in similar ways. Even within a language, the word may be interpreted very differently from one generation and one location to the next. Cheshire is very aware of the need for a brand to respond to these subtleties, but believes there is a desire for home – "an emotional engine" – that calls for a response:

> It's quite different from person to person, but the emotional engine is the same across the world. In China, "better homes, better lives" is about moving up the social scale and providing a room for your one child to then study and do more, whereas in a Western home, it's about creating a place where your children are safe and an entertaining hub for your family and friends. A kitchen in a Western home is much more about sharing – whereas the Chinese kitchen is tiny, it's much more about food production. I think one of the challenges for us is to try to get a broader set of issues into what better homes means. It doesn't just mean more stuff; for many consumers it means one that's cheaper to run. It's about trying to understand what sort of thing consumers are interested in, and work out how you can help them do it – because it's them doing it not us.

Cheshire is under no illusion about the complexity of desire. In his efforts to understand Kingfisher's consumers, he asks questions about their geographical, cultural and economic context, as we've seen, but also about their emotional state: what will make them feel good about themselves.

> Going back to energy efficiency, the positive consumer desire is for a warm home: they're very aware of the economics of it, but the powerful insight is that they just want to feel better in it. Trying to communicate this broader view of desire, including their desire to feel good about themselves and to say to other people that they've done the right thing, is absolutely fundamental for a brand.

I am intrigued by Cheshire's focus on the desire of people to do the right thing, and challenge him: is this really an important factor for consumers? "People routinely underestimate how essentially decent the vast majority of mankind is", he replies.[17]

C H A L L E N G E   Y O U R   B R A N D

- How does your brand affect people's sense of who they are?
- What role could your brand play in strengthening relationships?
- How could you help to bring people together in authentic ways?

Giving, not just getting

So far, in asking how brands can respond to the desire for community, we have looked at the importance of the right context for exchange, and in particular the advantage of a space designed by those who will use it. But what about the attitudes of people towards each other in that space, and even outside it? Can brands help to shape the very way in which we treat each other? Do they have a role in our relationships?

A brand strategy based on supporting people to be good to one another may sound like a lead balloon. It's too worthy, not sexy enough. But the psychoanalyst and essayist Adam Phillips asserts that there is real pleasure to be had in being kind to other people, pure and simple. As he sees it, our assumption that self-interest is the most natural state for mankind is depriving us of one of the things we desire most: to experience the wellbeing of those around us. "I think the primary longing is for that communal pleasure. That's the real thing. I think everybody feels that."[18]

Phillips explains that the desire to give and receive pleasure was strongly recognized by the Stoics (for a couple of hundred years before and after the life of Christ) but, he argues, it has been lost since. "Stoics were famously self-reliant, but the self on which a Stoic relied was not singular but communal", he explains.[19] They actually drew pleasure from kindness, Phillips argues, perceiving it as "a fount of happiness that 'expanded the soul'". Then along came post-Augustinian Christianity which, Phillips says, linked kindness, "disastrously", to self-sacrifice.[20] Much later, he continues, "prophets" of capitalism like Adam Smith proposed that individual desires could be turned to public benefit – but they didn't see public benefit as a desire in itself.

Theologians may not agree with Phillips' rather thinly evidenced account of Christian kindness. Ian Christie, a Research Fellow at the University of Surrey's Centre for Environmental Strategy and an advisor for the think tank on religion and society Theos, maintains that Christian giving is characterized by unconditionality: you do as you would have others do to you, whatever the personal consequences. Like Phillips, he points towards other socio-political trends that might explain any potential decrease in instances of human kindness, such as the emphasis in contemporary Western society on individual rights and autonomy.[21]

It's not easy to envision a shift towards a culture in which acts of kindness are understood to be truly rewarding, particularly in a society accustomed to idioms like "There's no such thing as a free lunch". But if a religion can establish a culture in which people find both moments of fun and a long-lasting sense of wellbeing in making other people happy, there is no reason why a brand shouldn't strive to do the same. Brands bring together lifestyle aspirations and cultural values in a way that has much in common with religions. Both aim to influence social norms and behaviors. What's more, the rise of a values-based market economy – emphasizing fair trade and environmental responsibility, for instance – brings these two mechanisms for social guidance even closer. It's important to remember that the fair-trade movement started out at the back of churches. "There certainly is a huge Christian market economy in the US", observes Christie. "If you are deliberately choosing to purchase from a Christian outlet, it's because you want your purchases to be consistent with your denomination and the values you have. You can imagine this trend going way beyond a religious motivation."

If people do look to brands to reinforce their sense of self, then one that is consistent with their values will have much greater traction. As Dr Rachel Howell, a researcher on consumer values and motivation at Aberystwyth University, observes, "People will feel a sense of personal integrity when acting in accordance with their values of social justice, community, or frugality".[22] Howell refers to several studies offering evidence that integrity motivates lifestyle choices.[23]

But even with the rise of values-based economies, it can be difficult to envision a successful brand strategy with kindness and generosity at its heart. Offers of "buy one get one free" entice consumers to buy products that weren't on their shopping list. Most prizes and freebies can only be claimed once a minimum amount has been spent. Even peer-to-peer sponsorship sites like JustGiving draw criticism for taking a 5 per cent cut from each donation.[24]

But the seeds of a new approach may already be in the ground. Philanthropy is drawing new interest from entrepreneurs with innovative approaches. Take Believe.in, a rival to JustGiving, backed by Index Ventures and Greylock Partners. Its mission statement pitch begins, "We believe people are good and care about making a positive impact." This may sound like a campaign for social justice, but make no mistake: Believe.in is a for-profit enterprise. It makes money through creating technology to help charities make better use of the web to build their profile and develop communities, alongside which it offers a free service to donors and charities, with no transaction, processing or annual membership fees. The way in which people give their money is subject to another rising trend: impact analysis, based on both quantitative and qualitative feedback.[25] Philanthropists don't just want to sign off cheques; they want to witness the change they have created. Of course, the returns on investment will rarely fit in with short-term quarterly figures – but one of the most influential people in philanthropy today doesn't consider this an obstacle.

Jacqueline Novogratz, founder-CEO of the non-profit Acumen Fund, advocates a new wave of philanthropy which offers long-term returns on investment, if funders are willing to leave their money with recipients for as many as ten or fifteen years. Novogratz calls this "patient capital" and believes it is the future of traditional aid. It means the onus to find solutions is not with the giver but with the receiver, who, through the transaction, becomes an entrepreneur with a mission – which might be to find a way to improve local health or sanitation, or protect crops from pests. The real value, for Novogratz, is in the recognition of mutual responsibility that such an exchange represents. In her words, "What we really yearn for as human beings is to be visible to each other."[26]

Ian Christie believes there could be a significant opportunity for brands in developing an approach based on long-term investment. In emerging economies, he says, people are moving from an underclass where they need to spend most of their time saving (if, indeed, they can escape debt), to a middle class in which they spend, or invest, what they have saved. This shift can happen over a lifetime or over generations. Christie observes that where they spend – as in the "developed" economies – is rarely the same place as where they save. "Brands that can invent themselves as homes of long-term investment and saving, and tie this in to your consumption, would offer a much more satisfying, meaningful relationship than people have with banks as we know them", he argues. This would work most effectively if the brand reinvests the money that you, as the saver, entrust to them in an intelligent way – that is, in a way that aligns with your values (ideally, with values supporting sustainability). For instance, the brand could invest your money back into your community, and share evidence of its impact through stories of transformation that really speak to you.

Community-based business models are on the rise. The current trend for peer-to-peer lending and sharing, or "collaborative consumption" – through the likes of Airbnb (the accommodation network), Zipcar (the car-sharing platform) and Taskrabbit (the errands and deliveries club) – is inspiring brands to look for innovative inroads into these new counter-high-street economies. Joanna Lumley was the face of "Shwopping", a campaign through which British retailer Marks and Spencer urged consumers to donate unwanted clothes, either in store, at work or through the retailer's partnership with Oxfam charity shops.

An awareness of the power of this trend is evident in Coca-Cola's "Share a Coke" campaign, which invites consumers "to share a moment of happiness with friends, family and loved ones". The campaign attracts attention by swapping the brand's well-known logo with 250 of the most popular names in Britain. Calling someone by name is a very powerful device, and the foundation of any personal relationship. Of course, it's only a start: establishing a strong bond takes time and emotional investment, and this is what Coca-Cola points towards through the invitation to share. It does beg the question: what more can Coca-Cola offer to support people in creating these moments of happiness, beyond its iconic brand platform?

This guide aims to help brands avoid shallow offers: ones that dress up their merchandise in promises of some greater wellbeing. Brands with the ambition to help their audience to feel connected, share and give must ask how they can best go about it, and what value they can bring. The reward will be lasting recognition.

CHALLENGE YOUR BRAND

- How could your brand nurture a culture of caring and sharing?
- What stories and rituals could you draw upon to enrich relationships?
- How can you help people to invest in the future of their community?

Desire-led brands in action

To recap, how can brands respond to our desire for community?

For one, they can help to bring people together in groups where they can share their passions and develop their interests. It's a much more binding offer than a selection of merchandise, and there is a business case for it. Just compare the one-off price of a t-shirt or scarf – which rarely accounts for the environmental or social costs of production – to the fee and profit margins of membership to a great space or society that people can feel proud to identify with.

Brands can work with people to create new spaces and platforms in which they can exchange ideas and build trust through trading skills. If we feel fondness and loyalty for the local café where we've had a few good chats in the past, how much more of a connection will we feel to a place we've helped to shape, and in which we can share anything we choose?

Even more powerfully, brands can influence the way in which we treat each other, endorsing new cultures and behaviors. Kindness might prove a whole realm to explore. If a brand can help someone to be so bold as to simply enjoy making someone else smile, it could become the heart of many anecdotes.

Here are three case studies to explore how some brands are trying and testing the potential of community. Each of these illustrates some aspects of the D – C – B – A approach to brand strategy which were set out in the Introduction. An ideal application of this approach, the brand begins by seeking a better understanding of desire: in this case, the desire for community. The brand would then use these insights to define its culture. Others would come to recognize this as integral to its character: its understanding of the desire for community would be at the heart of everything it says and does. The brand uses its conversations to create actions responding to this desire, in collaboration with its audience.

I explore the approach of each brand below, keeping these key questions in mind:

- How has this brand developed its understanding of the desire for community?
- How has it involved its audience in the process, and how does it keep them engaged?
- How has this engagement helped the brand find its way forward?

Case studies

1   Ansaar Management Company

In 2010, one-fifth of the total land area of Pakistan was covered in flood water following heavy monsoon rains in the Indus River basin. The UN Secretary General at the time, Ban Ki-Moon, called it the worst natural disaster he had ever seen: 20 million people were affected by loss of property, infrastructure, crops and business; 2000 lost their lives. Since then, there have been more floods, and land prices have shot up. The people affected have built makeshift settlements, known as *katchi abadis,* and are working to meet basic requirements, from graveyard walls and paved places for funerals, to clean water, toilets and ablution facilities. In March 2013, the provincial government of Punjab formally recognized the existence of over 3400 of these settlements, and accorded land rights to some 1.7 million inhabitants.[27] This is not a scalable solution, however, and the need for affordable housing for at least another 18 million is indisputable. Moreover, shelter and the right to land are only ever going to be part of the answer. There are economies to rebuild, cultures and lifestyles to preserve, and the need to re-establish trust so that people can share or trade limited resources.

Ansaar Management Company [AMC], a for-profit social enterprise, believes it has a role to play in all of this. Its aim is not just to provide affordable housing solutions to the lower income segments of the Pakistani population, but also to "create vibrant and empowered communities where the average citizen can raise a family". Moreover, AMC sets out to improve the existing lifestyles of the clients it rehouses, "while not compromising their indigenous way of life". Through rigorous consultation and co-creation processes, the residents are treated "as empowered contributors", rather than as passive beneficiaries. This, the company claims, creates "a firm sense of ownership within the community".[28]

The business model is innovative. While the development is not cooperatively owned, the residents collectively contribute the cost of a ten-acre parcel of land for the construction of the project, and at least one member of each household is required to help build their own house. According to AMC, this financial contribution and the dedication of labor or masonry skills are key to the development of a strong sense of community.

Fundamental to this design process is that the residents are selected before the settlement is built. AMC targets people in a certain income band (US $95-235 per month) who have lost their home during the floods; the selection process also stipulates that they must be landless. One of the most important conditions for selection, also stipulated in the contract, is that the resident has to agree to continuous self-occupancy of the allotted home, and neither to sub-let nor to sell the property. The social contract to which they sign up is not unlike the citizenship offered by a state – although it lasts just three years. During that time, the residents must agree to offer 24 days of community service a year, to send their children to school and to contribute Rs 300 a month to a fund managed by the residents themselves to maintain common facilities, such as waste management and horticulture, and for any other use as the community sees fit, through its democratically elected governing body.

Once this three-year development period is up, the land and home is transferred to the resident, unencumbered by any condition, and they can do with it as they see fit. Whether or not they choose to stay on, and whether they continue to develop their community and build on its social, environmental and economic assets, is a clear test of success for AMC.

So what does this all look like on the ground? One example of AMC's work is the Pakpur Noor Ghazi Village, an eight-acre settlement of 100 houses, about 12km from Muzaffargarh, a city in southwestern Punjab. It sits on the banks of the Chenab River, and between this and the Indus. A double water source is great for the sweet mangoes and nuts for which the city is known – and for other local crops including wheat, cotton and sugarcane – but it means that this region is particularly hard hit by flooding.

Far beyond just bricks and mortar, this village has a rich social infrastructure – made possible through engagement of the community to manage and maintain the facilities, and their collaboration with other local organizations. Governance is supported by the Pakpur Foundation, a forum of academics, policy makers, business leaders and development experts that works with non-profit organizations to develop solutions to social problems. A primary school run by the Progressive Education Network draws 200 students from within and outside the community, almost half of them female. Residents can also develop professional skills in textiles and tailoring through an institute funded by the Punjab Vocational Training Council; 75 women from the village were enrolled in January 2013. Basic health care is also available and was essential in fighting water-borne disease following the floods; each community member spends approximately Rs 100 per month on this facility. A plant converts 80 liters of salt water to drinking water for each household every day. There's also a calf-fattening unit, six recreational parks and a prayer hall. All these facilities are managed by the community, creating jobs in maintenance and service provision – from waste management to security – with 90 per cent of those employed recruited within the community.

A report by the Pakpur Foundation on the development of the project, from August 2010 to January 2013, notes that:

> The insistence on having residents input two of their most precious resources – time and money – into the construction of their home so that they felt connected to and vested into their future abodes was a key difference in this project compared to similar rehabilitation projects. Whereas similar projects in the area are either sitting vacant or in dilapidated condition (such as the Al-Khair Model Village, Village Meeran Mullah), the result in Noorghazi has been at least 90 per cent occupancy since inception.[29]

By involving the residents from the outset of the development of the project, AMC was able to learn about their understanding of the resources that would help them to establish a strong community. Their involvement is key to the success of the project throughout, including the solutions to any problems that arise, as the Director of Development Amjad Aslam describes below.

Preliminary research by AMC showed that the value of a home in the settlement had grown by 35 per cent from 2011-13, and that the value of the land surrounding the community had grown by 300 per cent, from Rs 300,000 per acre to Rs 1.2 million per acre. In a pre-sale study conducted in 2013, AMC estimated that at least 80 per cent of the residents would stay in their homes.

A CONVERSATION WITH AMJAD ASLAM, DIRECTOR OF DEVELOPMENT AT AMC

Amjad Aslam is a founding director of AMC, and leads its marketing and community development efforts. He has over 20 years of experience leading marketing and communication portfolios in private, public and non-profit organizations, including the World Wide Fund for Nature, where he came to the conclusion that a core socio-economic problem for the underprivileged people of Pakistan is lack of adequate housing and strong communities. I asked him how important it is that AMC interacts with its residents and understands what they want.[30]

Every sensible marketing person will tell you that the most important element for a brand is communication with its customers and stakeholders. I've been working in AMC since its inception, three years ago. We are such a young organization that the brand is not yet very clear. What we do as an organization, the work itself – this is the brand. There are no communications beyond that, and I think this is true for any small organization. I look after three portfolios and seven developments, and my role is sales and marketing, which means marketing the projects themselves.

When we talk about brand, when we talk about image, we are talking about what we want to be in the minds of our customers. We ask, what are our deliverables and how we can deliver them? That is our brand. Our customers will become our brand ambassadors. They will say they believe in us, because whatever we say we will deliver, we do.

How do you want to be perceived by your audience?

By those people who live in our developments, we want to be seen as people who are there to facilitate a change. That change is the difference between the way in which they were living before they were a resident, and their life. We are a change-maker, and a change-maker is not necessarily your friend, because he or she has to intervene. You can intervene as a facilitator, and you can intervene as a leader. For us, it is extremely important that our residents see us in a leadership role.

Why is leadership so important to AMC?

Because we are dealing with disenfranchised and marginalized people: they feel and believe that they cannot be a part of the change. They see their role in life as reactive: responding to a situation beyond their control. As a leader, we want to instill in them that, together, we are powerful and meaningful. Our systems of change at AMC are very democratic, and so we offer leadership, but change has to come through the residents themselves.

How do you develop trust as leaders?

Leadership is what you do, and doing what you say. At Noor Ghazi, for the first six months, a group of people – the future residents, the engineers and civil construction technicians, and AMC's community development people – were all living on the site; they were all in tents. When, after one and a half years, the construction people exited, the community development people carried on living there alongside the residents for another two and a half years. They were interacting with them on a daily basis, sitting down with them, helping them to organize bills, to develop councils, to deal with floods. All this meant that these people are not merely facilitators, they are also leaders.

You talk about leadership, but how much time do you spend listening to your audience? How important is it to you to find out what they want?

For us, it starts by listening. Every region has its own reality, its own living style. For instance, our developments in Lahore have a courtyard in the front of the house. When we went to the rural areas, we found that we needed to change the design, because our beneficiaries wanted the courtyard behind the house.

Listening is the most important element for AMC, because in a way we are foreigners for them. Our reality has to be in tandem with their reality. Unless we understand their reality, our work has no legs to stand on. Before we even choose a site for development, we start by asking, "What do you require? Do you want a school, or a mosque...?"

Our development plans are block-based: 22 houses constitute one block, and so there is a community within a community. We are dealing with individuals as householders, and then with each block development committee, who sit down and talk to each other every week. In that meeting every week, we are listening. Then there is a fortnightly community-wide meeting, and so there is constant interaction between ourselves and the beneficiaries.

If a resident comes to us and says that he or she has a problem with a neighbor, then we ask them to file a complaint: there is an open process. We don't just react on the spot. This is how we are establishing our brand: by building trust through our actions.

We haven't exited from any project as yet: we are still there, talking to people. I personally know each and every resident.

Is it difficult for a business to build trust in Pakistan?

Yes. Pakistan has problems of corruption. In any project, anything that you do, you can speed up things by giving the Government money, and AMC refuses to do that. We want to show that people can do business in Pakistan without being corrupt.

It's important to understand that the concept of social enterprise is very new here. Traditionally, social development is considered to be the purview of the Government: it is supposed to provide health, education and welfare. Whereas the Government looks at macro-level problems, the model for local development has always been philanthropy. This model is very well developed through organizations like WWF, and international bodies like the UNDP. They have done a lot of good work in Pakistan, and they are trusted; but they do have their own agenda, and their managerial processes mean that perhaps 25 per cent of the funds for a project, such as sanitation, are swallowed in overheads and fees.

We are a profit-making enterprise, and we work with non-profit partners – which include government bodies, other developers and service providers. For instance, in a development, all the civil and social infrastructure is built by us – the school is built by us, but we do not run it: that is the role of one of our partners. These non-profit organizations firmly believe that an enterprise that is profit-oriented will never act justly. How can it help people, when its motive is to profit from them? We have to go out and explain our model, which is absolutely new here. And so building trust through delivery is a very integral part of our brand. The brand that we want to establish is the fact that we do deliver on our side of any contract.

We don't spend any money on advertising, not a single rupee. We are very aware that all our money comes from the customer, and they are our beneficiary. We owe to them everything we do, and so we look for ways to save money all the time. Every single penny we can save is a penny our beneficiaries can invest. If ever we take a car, we fill it with four people. We go and meet people, talk to them, get them to understand us.

As we see it, the proof of the pudding is in eating it. We have been very fortunate that we have done good work on the ground. Someone can always take the pudding and say "taste it", but it was the model itself that got people intrigued.

In what way do you think AMC has strengthened the community in Noor Ghazi?

You may be aware that Pakistan has a problem with religion, in the sense that there are quite a number of sects within Islam, and there are people who are non-Muslims as well. It's like the Protestants and Catholics at the time of Queen Elizabeth I: this is where we are now. One of our great achievements is that we have managed to bring people of multiple denominations together, living in one place, and we have convinced them to pray together. We have convinced them to use the mosque together, jointly, and I feel that is an enormous success. There are also non-Muslims, actually living side by side with Muslims. It's difficult to communicate the significance of this to someone from outside of Pakistan.

The way we went about it was to say there would be only one mosque. This was our leadership. Then we waited for the problems to arise. We anticipated them, but we did not put preventative schemes in place. We waited until the problems arose, and that gave us the opportunity to ask people why they were so gung-ho about it. Because people were very sensitive to these issues, they became very vocal. They talked to each other in group discussion, after group discussion, after group discussion.

In Islam we have a prayer leader: one person who stands in front and guides the practice. We suggested that you rotate that person leading the prayers – from one sect to another. We said there will not be a resident prayer leader, but that for festivities and special occasions, they can be hired for that specific time. They are hired by the community, with consensus, and they have to be non-denominational. Development problems have a human side and a technical side. You need a place to pray and a person to lead the prayer, those things have to be in place. But in order to satisfy the human side, you have to create a solution together.

What do you do when things go wrong?

If a problem arises, we take it very seriously. There are three main things that cause problems: criminal activities, social ills and lifestyle concerns. If a crime is committed, it is not our role to deal with it: we call the police. However, the AMC staff there actually are involved in the criminal justice procedures, as a representative of the community. We help to make sure there are no injustices done.

If there is a social ill – such as truancy, when kids aren't going to school – we work alongside the school. Every day the school attendance is sent to AMC, and if the kid from house number 11 is absent, a staff member will go and enquire why. If needs be, the problem can be raised in a committee meeting. In one case, a kid was working for his father – a real issue to which we have listened and helped to create a solution.

Then there are lifestyle issues. Lots of young children used to go about barefoot. It's not a social ill, but it requires an intervention. That intervention is done by asking questions: why is your child not wearing footwear? Before we do community development, we do community appreciation: we analyze their habits. We call this KAP analysis, studying knowledge, attitudes and practice. There's also belief analysis: the community might have a practice that impedes development, and so we ask, what is their belief? For example, a lot of people believe that tap water is not good for you. In many places the water is actually fine, but if you believe it isn't, that is a problem. We also do socio-economic analysis. We know the assets of our communities, and we revisit the data to find out if their circumstances are improving.

How will you know if the project has been a success, after the initial development phase is over?

We are in the business of change, and so if our communities do not change, our business and brand also stand still. For AMC, it's not about building a house, and it's not putting a person in a house, and it's not sending children to school: it's bringing about a change. The indicators of that change are the people themselves; if they are benefiting from that change, it is evident that they will talk about it. But they will only talk about it, and our role in it, if they feel we have delivered what we promised. They have to feel that their environment is better. Each person is interacting with their world, their immediate surroundings, and so the change has to be very visible to them.

When the people of Noor Ghazi first moved in, none of them had personal transport – not even a bicycle. But then some of them began to buy motorbikes and scooters. Now, as they drive around, people ask them how their economic conditions have changed. If we have succeeded, they will mention us in their story.

Our website will also be very important. We intend to use it as a living document, where people can post their stories and others can watch their lives unfold. The testimonials of our community can play a big role in developing our brand.

Finally, we haven't done this yet, but we want to invite people from the media to come and visit the sites, to be our guest, and meet the people living there. They will see for themselves.

2   Made in the Lower East Side

South of 14th Street, east of Bowery, north of Brooklyn Bridge, and west of East River: these are the boundaries of Manhattan's Lower East Side, New York. It's a community with a diverse population that attracts many entrepreneurs: fashion designers, magazine producers, arts teachers – people whose creativity and commercial success depends on a rich network of collaborators and consumers. They need space to trade or exhibit, but are unlikely to have the funds to lease a property, let alone invest in one. Around them, shops thrive in the day and bars buzz at night – but when they close, they leave a space that could be put to use. This is the opportunity spotted by the local enterprise Made in the Lower East Side (miLES).

miLES aims to do for storefronts what Airbnb has done for spare rooms, or Zipcar for vehicles: unleash the social and economic potential of underused resources. But its focus is on a particular community and it recognizes that its primary resource is not so much the space as what the people in it do with it.

miLES began by asking people in this community what they were looking for, prompting them to think about the potential of their area, their own aspirations and what they would need to fulfil them. It brandished huge posters saying, "Lower East Side is underused. 212 vacant spaces = 212 possibilities. What would you do with an empty space?" The outreach process comprised dialogues with community groups and influencers, individual interviews, role play, shadowing and diary-writing, and the results were shared via blog, print media and live "townhall" feedback events.[31] In a video posted on YouTube,[32] Chelsea Campbell, who calls herself an Experience Designer, says that she'd like to do a live magazine, and Sheena Sood imagines a pop-up launch event for her fashion brand.

The business model has various components. To open up the storefronts, miLES forms partnerships with their lease-holders, offering a full service in which it examines the space and works out potential applications, addresses any safety hazards, restructures it for particular uses, and helps to bring in new audiences. For instance, Parkside Lounge, a bar on East Houston Street, is now available to rent for performance or rehearsal sessions on weekday afternoons, at a rate of $100 for a five-hour session. It's a 1000 square foot space, with wifi, a stage, seating for 77 people, complete with drums, a keyboard and amplifiers for guitar and bass. Another space is Evany, an 800 square foot boutique, ideal for pop-up shops and events such as evening classes or exhibitions.

miLES offers people with ideas help to find the right space to display or prototype a project, or run an event. Importantly, it also brings all the various pop-up initiatives together under one common brand, and markets them. Its own brand grows through the enthusiasm and involvement of its collaborators, and it promotes their events through its own networks. Locals can either rent a space on a one-off basis or apply to become a "Co-Working Member", buying the right to work in miLES storefronts during the week, discounted entry to related events and premium rates on rental of the spaces.

What this brand communicates above all is the potential of collective creativity to transform a community: its aim is to attract those it can empower. Clearly, the more people it meets and the more projects it can help get off the ground, the more demand it will generate for the spaces it offers. Everything about the brand invites resourcefulness and a "do it ourselves" approach. The logo is inspired by a simple rubber stamp, and the brand's key messages are scrawled in felt-tip pen on cardboard. Its declared mission is "to create vibrant community spaces, offer a temporary home for emerging projects, and provide inclusive economic opportunities for the neighborhood".[33]

The minds behind miLES also recognize the potential of their business to grow through strengthening its network and, in particular, by supporting the entrepreneurs whose creative endeavors are its fuel. Beyond one-off events, they are encouraging more collaboration and bringing people together to share skills through a series of workshops and a mentoring network. The mentors are marketed as "Sifus", a Cantonese term for someone who masters a particular skill.

miLES won a One Prize 2012 award for urban design. The jury noted that they were impressed by its "dedication to the involvement of multiple stakeholders, to its positive impact on the neighborhood, its bottom up approach and compelling feasibility".[34] As Steven Jacobs, a professor in urban planning at New York University, observes, the miLES team understands that "for this program to be truly successful and take root here, it must address the needs of building owners, business owners and local residents and visitors."

3   Heineken UK

Communities have come together over beer for centuries, in monasteries, taverns, bars and clubs. It has always been about more than just the drink.

In the UK's age-old pub culture, it's the sense of home from home: the tales told by the fire; the round of pints that friends offer each other; the gossip, jokes and songs; the celebrated occasions with everyone squeezed in front of the same screen – from football matches to the pomp and circumstance of royal celebrations. Without community, a lager falls a bit flat.

Of course, pubs don't always contribute to communities in a positive way. They can be centers of violence, discrimination and alcohol abuse. If healthy communities are important to any business, they are important to a brewer. But getting close to a community is a challenge for mainstream drinks manufacturers and the owners of pub chains. The communication campaigns of many drinks brands rely on sponsorship of sporting events and music festivals, where they monopolize the bars and any other platform with their logo. This brings visibility, and perhaps an association with the interests and culture of the people it wants to reach, but it does little to strengthen the community itself.

Such brands are also increasingly subject to criticism, where communities suffer from the ill effects of alcohol abuse, and to public calls for responsibility. Each instance of criticism could be recognized as an invitation to have a more meaningful conversation with that community about what it wants from its local hub: not just the choice of drinks, but the space itself, its culture, and the resources it can contribute.

As Stefan Orlowski, Chair of the UK Marketplace Leadership Team for the brewer Heineken from January 2012 to May 2013 and now Regional President of Heineken Americas, states on the website of UK non-profit Business in the Community: "As an alcohol company we are very much under the spotlight of public scrutiny and we recognize our duty to demonstrate responsible behaviour [sic] and earn our right to be a respected brand in society."[35]

In light of this, Heineken UK has developed a new business model, to enable it to interact more closely with those people at the heart of the industry: the pub landlords and ladies. The brand has established a leasing scheme, under the banner Star Pubs & Bars, to support entrepreneurs in leasing and running their own pub. Heineken offers start-up funding and training, and the tenant, or lessee, of the pub brings their knowledge of the local community. Under this scheme, Heineken has now bought and leased over 1300 UK pubs. In 2013, this mainstream brand won both the

Asda Enterprise Growth Award and a Business in the Community Award, recognizing the double win here – both for the future of Heineken's brand and for the communities in which it invests.

The declared aim of Star Pubs & Bars is "to be the most successful and sustainable leased pub business in the UK": a mission statement that comes with an important qualifier. "[W]e know we can't do this alone. That's why we aim to attract and develop outstanding talent and support our lessee partners with industry-leading retail advice."[36]

The lessee is offered support to plan and develop the business, training programs to ensure good management, financial investment in the refurbishment and support with the supply chain to keep costs low, including energy saving measures. Tenants can terminate a lease with three months' notice and additional investment is on offer to help with early cash flow.

Orlowski adds: "We invest in our pubs and in developing the skills of the lessees, who are running them to create pubs people love. We're constantly looking at ways to add value to lessees and make our partnerships stronger."

One beneficiary of the scheme is Graham Anderson, a life-long resident of Bristol who had worked in pubs and managed them for over 15 years. Anderson felt there was "a massive gap" in his neighborhood, Henleaze, "for a quality local serving great food".[37] He had spotted a pub in need of new ownership, but was held back by the upfront costs and financial risks of taking it over.

Heineken's Star Pubs & Bars scheme has enabled Anderson to build a business at the Eastfield Inn. Crucially, he was involved in developing the terms of the lease and also in the pub's refurbishment. "We have put together a deal that works for us both and they have been very receptive to my input into the redesign of the Eastfield Inn. It's great to start out with a pub that is just as I want it." His revenue will be enhanced by an extra space for functions, thanks to a redesign of the conservatory as a year-round venue.

Business in the Community commends the scheme for supporting new enterprises that employ 13,000 people, generating a 30-100 per cent return on investment for lessees and helping them to save up to 40 per cent on energy supply and 4 per cent on building work. It's a commercial success for Heineken too: in 2012, the net profit of Star Pubs & Bars grew by 1.6 per cent, it reported the highest sales of beer in the pub market and generated the highest average sales turnovers of any national UK leased pub estate.[38]

So how is the Eastfield Inn shaping up as a community hub? A reviewer in the *Bristol Post* writes, "The new-look Eastfield Inn has finally realized its potential as a family-friendly local serving unpretentious, good quality food. Having one of the biggest and best beer gardens in Bristol is an added bonus." He also emphasizes the opportunities the pub has created for other local businesses: "…the kitchen uses a number of quality local suppliers including Ruby & White butchers and Joe's Bakery, whilst desserts are made locally by Absolutely Cakes."[39] The Inn's Facebook page regularly posts events, from football and tennis matches to pub quizzes and live music. And the cricket club Henleaze Old Boys credits Anderson – who happens to be one of its front line bowlers – for providing "the team with cracking after-match sandwiches and Man of the Match pints…"[40] You can guess which beer they are drinking.

chapter 2
Adventure

Adventure is the desire to explore and discover, and through this to challenge ourselves and grow. It's a desire we experience from our earliest days. Think how readily children create their own adventures, making games out of exploration and discovery. They venture into forbidden places, propelled by curiosity and uninhibited by the sense of risk we gain with experience. They build dens and hideaways, creating new realms in which they are in charge, and from which they can challenge the ways of the world. They dress up as doctors and soldiers, princesses and wizards, exploring their identity and the roles they could play in life. They probe about in realms they might later shy away from – pulling earthworms from the soil and examining them with more glee than squirm. The pleasure they find may have little to do with the worm itself – nor would they really want to wake up and find they're on the frontline. But through play, children expand their own horizons. They awaken and respond to the desire for adventure itself.

Of course, how we set about our adventures – where we go and what guides us – varies across geography, culture and generation. This is also true of child's play. Researchers in Taiwan observed that, in the 1970s, children primarily played outdoors, describing how they would use ingredients from their natural surroundings, such as coconut leaves to weave "grasshoppers" and make wind instruments. By contrast, the rise of kindergartens and nurseries to support parents working long hours meant that indoor play dominated in the 1990s – and construction materials like Lego and bricks were favored. Today, children increasingly learn and play using tablets and other digital media. Indoors or out, children experiment with their environment, exploring it and reimagining it.

If we think about desire as a force that causes us to reach out for things that stimulate our senses and engage our minds, then adventure is one of its most natural channels. The very word (from the Latin prefix ad, for "towards", and the verb venire, "to reach" or "to come") propels us into the future: what will come, and what we ourselves will, in time, become. As the French social scientist René Girard – whose theory of mimetic desire has influenced psychologists, neuroscientists and economists – put it: "all desire is a desire to be".[1]

It takes a combination of imagination and motivation to open ourselves up to the possibility of "becoming", welcoming and pursuing change in ourselves – our habits and attitudes – as well as in our surroundings. In some cases we begin by imagining where we might end up, and then take our first steps towards it. At other times we simply feel propelled to go out and explore, to follow our nose. In any case, we set out – as tourists and explorers, reporters and researchers, evangelists and imperialists – on a journey of personal development and worldly discovery.

There are of course many reasons to venture to new places: to find food and water; to reach safety; or to achieve a political or economic goal, such as expanding your empire or dominating an area rich in natural resources. But adventure also has an intrinsic value. In many cases, there is no particular reason to leave, no particular goal to pursue. The adventurer is drawn towards a new space in which to grow – rather like a plant seeking light.

This chapter explores the desire for adventure in its broadest sense. Travel is one response to it, but we also broaden our horizons through metaphorical journeys: we develop new skills or delve into a particular discipline; we try out ways of thinking and behaving, perhaps inspired by a culture or a person we admire; we push ourselves beyond our comfort zone by going into new social contexts or trying our hand at extreme sports. If we were to come back entirely the same, we'd likely be disappointed – and often we bring a token, from a tan to a medallion, to give others a sense of the experiences we've had and how we have changed. If adventure were to be associated with a particular ambition (although for many the very idea of a goal would be inhibiting enough to keep them at home) then this would be self-actualization: the highest rung on Abraham Maslow's pyramid. Maslow spoke of the desire to accomplish everything that one can and to become the most that one can be. Adventure doesn't necessarily come with the ambition Maslow evokes, and which we will explore in the section on Purpose in Chapter 4. I see "adventure" as an arrow fired off in a similar direction, but with a focus on enjoying the flight.

Living to tell the tale

The desire to develop your character, skills and potential, and the significance that many cultures accord to journeys of the mind and spirit, is shaped by thousands of years of storytelling. Tales of adventure passed down from one generation to the next help to define communities by creating common understandings of where we came from, who came before us and what shared values and intentions bind us together. As the renowned post-colonial literary theorist Edward Said wrote, "nations themselves are narrations".[2] He argued that people use stories "to assert their own identity and the existence of their own history". This link between identity and narrative is so powerful, he warned, that stories can also be a weapon, used to challenge, colonize and even efface the identity of others. Said offers many examples, among them the portrayal of Africa in Joseph Conrad's *Heart of Darkness* which, he argues, reflects neither Africa nor an experience of Africa. Instead, "an extraordinarily rich mix" of lore and writing about Africa, Conrad's own impressions of those texts, and narrative convention create "a politicized, ideologically saturated Africa". To most Europeans, Said goes on, reading *Heart of Darkness* was "as close as they came to Africa, and in that limited sense it was part of the European effort to hold on to, think about, plan for Africa."[3]

Narrative has such a formative power because in listening to the tales of others, we too go on a journey. As far as our powers of imagination are concerned, it doesn't seem to matter whether these tales are mythical, fictional or historical. Set off with Zheng He or with Harry Potter: on either journey it will be your own boundaries that you explore, and your own assumptions that are challenged. If, at some later stage, you embark

When we listen to the tales of others, we too go on a journey

on a (non-fictional) journey, you will move into the spaces that their adventures created in your imagination, by expanding your sense of what is both possible and desirable. If you have never travelled to Africa, what you perceive when you arrive will inevitably be shaped by the literature you have read, the music you have heard, the films you have seen.

When Western tourists travel to India in search of spiritual development, they are arguably engaging in a tradition of spiritual adventure that can be traced back 4000 years to the Ramayana, one of India's founding epics and a cornerstone of the Hindu faith. First told by the sage-poet Valmiki, according to tradition, it recounts the journey – the "ayana", which in Sanskrit means "advancing" – of Rama, the seventh incarnation of Lord Vishnu. It has all the elements you might expect in an adventure story, such as the kidnapping of Rama's beloved Sita by the demon-king Ravana, whom he has to overcome. But it is also the story of Rama's own spiritual and moral development. The Ramayana is told through the course of 24,000 verses, which were memorized by Valmiki's followers and passed down through public readings. These readings are still common in Indian villages and across South East Asia – and the desire to share these tales has not been side-lined by the rise of visual media. The Hindu scholar Ranchor Prime describes the Ramayana as "a staple of Indian cinema", and recalls how, in the late 1980s, a television serial based on the Ramayana, broadcast over 78 weeks, "brought the nation to a standstill for an hour each Sunday".[4]

Today, some of the most influential storytellers are brands. I don't just mean that J. K. Rowling, by virtue of spinning adventures, is a brand – although, through much marketing, including a ground-breaking website, she has become one. What I mean is that brands tell stories, and in doing so, introduce us to their culture and prompt us to imagine ourselves as players in their world.

CHALLENGE YOUR BRAND

- What opportunities for exploration and personal development does your brand offer?
- How do the stories you tell as a brand expand the horizons of your audience?
- How can you support individuals to tell their own tales of adventure?

The consumer fantasy

With the rise of consumerism, many brands have assumed the role of storyteller to show their audience aspirational realms to which the only key is consumption. The average man moves into a realm where he is considered a sex god by buying a deodorant, and the weary mother is transformed into a household goddess thanks to a detergent. These adverts sit comfortably alongside that epic of social aspiration – the soap opera, which gets its name from the sponsorship of soap manufacturers, such as Lever Brothers and Procter & Gamble. But the correlation between a brand's narrative and people's day-to-day adventures runs much deeper than this. Every brand offers to take its audience towards a better place – and must shape their aspirations in order to convince them to go down that road. The earlier they can begin to engage with an individual's ideals, the more potential they will have to shape their future choices, and so children can become prime targets for brand campaigns. Moreover, digital and social media offer brands more channels with which to interact with young people than ever before.

The American cultural critic Henry A. Giroux, holder of the Global TV Network Chair Professorship at McMaster University in Hamilton, Ontario, writes:

> Under the tutelage of Disney and other megacorporations, children have become an audience captive not only to traditional forms of media such as film, television and print, but even more so to the new digital media made readily accessible through mobile phones, PDAs, laptop computers and the Internet [sic]. The information, entertainment and cultural pedagogy disseminated by massive multimedia corporations have become central in shaping and influencing every waking moment of children's daily lives – all toward a lifetime of constant, unthinking consumption.

Giroux describes Disney as "a powerful example of the new corporate media at the beginning of the 21st century", which "like many other megacorporations ... continually expands its products and services to reach every available media platform". He refers to its brand image as:

> ...titanium-clad ... synonymous with a notion of childhood innocence and wholesome entertainment – that manages to deflect, if not

completely trounce, criticism at every turn. As an icon of American culture and middle-class family values, Disney actively appeals to both conscientious parents and youthful fantasies as it works hard to transform every child into a lifetime consumer of Disney products and ideas.[5]

Disney's primary tool for shaping the aspirations of children – through whatever platform or product – is the adventure story. Its approach is smart: the brand undergoes extensive research to find out what the children in its audience dream about and offers to make this "come true". Giroux describes how Disney uses "educators and anthropologists … to study all aspects of the culture and intimate lives of young boys, but to do so in a way that allows Disney to produce 'emotional hooks' that lure young boys into the wonderful world of corporate Disney in order to turn them into enthusiastic consumers." He cites in particular the work of an anthropologist called Kelly Peña, who was commissioned to spend time with boys aged 6-14, working out what makes them tick.[6] According to the *New York Times*, "Ms Peña, 45, told producers that boys identify with protagonists who try hard to grow. 'Winning isn't nearly as important to boys as Hollywood thinks,' she said." It's no accident – the reporter surmises – that the eponymous hero of the adventure series Aaron Stone, the first to air on Disney XD, is "a mediocre basketball player" with whom young boys are likely to identify.[7]

The difference between Disney's approach to desire and the one proposed in this book is that Disney only really offers one response to those dreams. It takes children on adventures that inevitably have a happy ending. Just as Pinocchio and Cinderella journey from the peripheries of society to the mainstream, and from "rags to riches", the message to these young minds is that they too will rise to social expectations, as consumers. First they'll go after the clothes and the looks, later the kingdom. Disney has been heavily criticized for the female role models it offers young girls. In 2013, it introduced the character Merida from the Pixar film *Brave* into its official "Princess" toy collection, but in doing so gave the bold adolescent a make-over, slimming her waist, accentuating her hips and breasts, shaping her eyebrows and darkening her eyelashes – in short, transforming her into its slim stereotype of a sexy young woman. The irony is that Merida herself was created in opposition to such stereotypes: she curses the femininity her mother would like to impose on her, ripping her dress to fire off one bulls-eye after another with her bow and arrow. A petition, signed by over 250,000 objectors, reads:

> The redesign of Merida in advance of her official induction to the Disney Princess collection does a tremendous disservice to the millions of children for whom Merida is an empowering role model who speaks to girls' capacity to be change agents in the world rather than just trophies to be admired. Moreover, by making her skinnier, sexier and more mature in appearance, you are sending a message to girls that the original, realistic, teenage-appearing version of Merida is inferior; that for girls and women to have value - to be recognized as true princesses - they must conform to a narrow definition of beauty.

The year before, in 2012, Disney had launched a campaign illustrating the "titanium-clad" approach that, for Giroux, makes the brand so powerful. The short film "I am a princess" sought to address a triple whammy of accusations: this sexualization of female role models for one, but also that Disney aims to transform children into consumers, and that it promotes individualism over community-based values. The film shows young girls of various ages, sizes and skin color going about idyllic activities: playing in meadows with friends, wrapping rugs over granny, playing chess with grandpa. The voice-over for the film says: "I am a princess. I believe in loyalty and trust. I think standing up for myself is important. I think that standing up for others is more important, but standing with others is most important." The accompanying micro-site describes the campaign as "a celebration of what it truly means to be a Princess today. To be brave. To be kind. To be generous and compassionate."

While claiming to emphasize solidarity and selfless ideals, the message at the heart of the film is nonetheless that young girls should set themselves apart as princesses, promoting the born privilege and elevated social status encapsulated by royalty. They are invited to express it through fine clothes, exclusive kingdoms and magic wands which grant them power over others. The campaign claims that the magic of the modern princess "is of her own design" and "is herself", and yet the film offers a clear image of what they should aspire to. One scene shows children enthralled by a large screen featuring Disney's take on Rapunzel – a pale skinned princess with long blonde hair, a tiny waist, a pink dress and a cleavage. Unsurprisingly, she escapes her tower to go on "a hilarious hair-raising journey" – which ends with her back at home with her royal parents, married to her true love (who at first seemed a bit of a truant but reveals during the film that he is indeed of equally privileged heritage) and living "happily ever after"...

CHALLENGE YOUR BRAND

- Who is the heroine or hero, and what qualities do they encourage in others?
- Where does their journey lead, and what do they learn on the way?
- Does the story end happily, and how does your brand define this?

Venturing beyond consumption

This critique of Disney is not intended as a warning against the role of brands in shaping our aspirations. They are a cultural vehicle like any other, and there is no reason why their influence should not be positive. Take Dove, the Unilever soap that has set out to confront narrow ideals of feminine beauty by promoting self-esteem. Instead of telling women that they need to become more beautiful, it urges them to recognize that they already are. The journey isn't towards enhanced beauty, but towards enhanced belief in the beauty you already possess.

A three-minute video campaign, the Dove Real Beauty Sketches, went viral on YouTube following its launch in April 2013. According to Unilever, it became the most watched video advertisement of all time in its first month, with more than 114 million views, in 25 languages. It tells the story of various women who are asked to sit for a portrait artist. There's an important twist: the artist – an experienced forensic trained by the FBI – can't see them, and instead sketches their faces by asking them questions about their own features: the shape and size of their forehead and jaw, their hair and freckles, and so on. He then produces another sketch, drawing on the way in which other people described them. The women are then showed the two contrasting portraits, and are visibly moved: the second portrait is invariably closer to the truth. Each woman has exaggerated any negatives she perceives in her own features, undermining her sense of her own beauty. They then reflect on the importance of self-esteem, and how much more effective they could be in various aspects of their lives if they could believe in their own beauty. "I should be more grateful of my natural beauty", says Florence, one of the women featured. "It impacts the choices and friends that we make, the jobs we apply for, how we treat our children. It impacts everything. It couldn't be more critical to your happiness."

The film's success demonstrates the appetite among women for a brand that affirms who they are, as opposed to telling them that they need to change. However, there is a gap between the offer encapsulated by the film – a journey for women towards an enhanced sense of their natural beauty – and what Dove ultimately offers its audience: a range of products. For millions of women inspired by the film to try to change the way they see themselves, it seems unlikely that yet another face cream or shampoo will prove the best aid. How will it help them to undo a lifetime's habit of looking in the mirror with dissatisfaction, or feeling envy at a friend's figure?

There is no reason why an adventure that begins with a brand should end in a neatly packaged purchase: there are other ways to do business. The desire we experience to grow as people and explore the world creates an opportunity for brands that offer to help us along our way. For a brand, the test of success is the never-ending journey. It isn't left by the wayside when the protagonist canters off; instead, it goes along as the faithful companion, the Sancho Panza.

Lab me up

Many adventures begin with an empowering gift: something that opens doors, reveals possibilities, or helps to overcome obstacles along the way. D'Artagnan is presented with 15 crowns, a horse and a letter of introduction by his father; James Bond goes to see Q to pick up his car and gadgets; the Master of Jordan College gives Lyra the all-knowing, all-telling alethiometer.

Brands can take up this role, providing access to the skills and tools that will help people expand their horizons. This is an obvious way for them to enter into the adventures of their audience, helping to shape their story from the start. Not only do they set themselves up as trusted friends and enablers, but the "key" they provide will act as a sort of memento on the journey. Each time it proves its worth, the brand is remembered. Moreover, the brand can then look for opportunities to enhance its original offer along the way, and be on hand as a go-to source of additional support.

What evidence is there that individuals might want or welcome such an offer? A report published in 2013 by the National Intelligence Council (NIC), the US center for long-term strategic analysis, identified individual empowerment as the most important of four "megatrends" that will shape the world in 2030. The report identifies a few contributing factors: an expanding global middle class – rising to over 2 billion people by 2030, according to conservative estimates; the growth of digital communications, and in particular the expansion of smartphones, reaching 65 per cent of the population of Africa; health improvements, including extended quality of life as people age and a shift in the global disease burden from communicable to non-communicable disease; and wider access to formal education among men and women, with particular reference to the Middle East and North Africa. The impact of these factors on the role of individuals in society will be so great, the authors argue, that it will usher in "a new era of 'democratization' at the international and domestic level".[8]

As individuals are offered more choice and flexibility in forging their future, demand will rise for services that can help them get started and find the right path. The authors of the NIC report identify knowledge and skills as the key tools they will need, and points to education as "both the motor and beneficiary" of this trend. In many parts of the world, this is a mixed sector, provided by a combination of government, private and non-profit bodies. Among them are some powerful brands, and little wonder: for individuals to trade their skills and knowledge, they often need a recognized stamp to prove they can deliver.

Universities like Oxford, Cambridge and the Sorbonne are among the world's oldest educational brands. Now at the top of the global league table for higher education is the California Institute of Technology, also known as Caltech. It was established with a gift of over $100,000 from a businessman in 1891, and is home to NASA's Jet Propulsion Laboratory: not bad as a launch pad for adventure. Which is pretty much how Caltech describes itself: "a world-renowned science and engineering research and education institution, where extraordinary faculty and students seek answers to complex questions, discover new knowledge, lead innovation, and transform our future". When the brand strategist Emily Buchholtz redesigned the website, her aim was to bring out the potential for journey and discovery, by making it read more like a story than a traditional website – with "striking images and a visual menu [to] draw the audience in and encourage exploration". If she was quick to latch on to the importance of adventure to Caltech's brand, it may be because her own journey towards a career in brand strategy began with a passion for rock-climbing in the Sierras and Cascades. "I wanted to share the amazing discoveries, explorations, and stories that shape our world", she recounts. "I searched for a way to become a 'professional storyteller' and found it as a Brand Strategist."[9]

The landscape for education is changing, as digital media and big data transform how we share and store ideas and knowledge. Traditional universities are having to find ways to compete with the rise of massive online open courses, or "MOOCs", that appeal to millions of students from across the world. More adults are also looking to develop their knowledge and skills outside of formal systems for higher education, through evening and weekend classes, residential courses, as well as online tools, creating a major opportunity for brands outside the educational sector. Attitudes towards adult learning are also changing. The long-held belief that childhood was the prime time for learning and that "the mind fossilizes as it ages" are being challenged by neurologists. "A few decades ago, few neuroscientists would have agreed that adults can rival the learning talents of children. But we needn't be so defeatists. The mature brain, it turns out, is more supple than anyone thought", writes David Robson in the *New Scientist*. With reference to the work of Gary Marcus at New York University and Arthur Kramer at the University of Illinois, he shows that scientists now understand how to accelerate knowledge and skill acquisition in adults. Mild exercise can help, according to Arthur Kramer, who found a 30–40 minute walk a few times a week increased the attention and synaptic connections of senior citizens. Trying your hand at new disciplines, and switching from one to the other – as opposed to striving for perfection – has also been found to increase an adult's aptitude to learn, Robson writes. "It seems that jumping between skills makes your mind work a little harder when applying what you've learned, helping you to retain the knowledge in the long term."

As opportunities to learn proliferate, with access to vast digital libraries as well as new tuition tools and methodologies, people will look for support to decide how best to use their time and the resources available. Which disciplines will set them up best for life, and what skills will they need? Trend-hunter and brand anthropologist Jody Turner, owner and founder of the strategic innovation company Culture of Future, believes there is a role for brands that can help the next generation orientate itself. She observes the emergence of a new culture, based on finding new pathways through huge amounts of information, and taking what you need with you.

"We're in a time of learning and growing", Turner explains. "Through global [digital] media, we have the opportunity to use the world as our pallet: we are upping our mass IQ. It's not just about the academic view. We can pick information from various places and make sense of it: curating, synthesizing, sense-mapping for other people."

Turner argues that everyone has the opportunity to become such a curator and shaper of ideas, and that young people naturally are. Those brands that can support them to share information and innovate will be able to create new arenas for these minds to try out new tricks – new laboratories for experimentation: "It's the accelerator generation. They're labbing up. It's the brands that open up to these brilliant people, the ones that invite the tech stars in, that will succeed – [the ones that] help you to create what you want."

Take the James Dyson Foundation, which – according to its own mission statement – "encourages young people to think differently, make mistakes and invent". It does this through support for promising design engineers, with bursaries for students in the US, the UK and South East Asia, and through partnerships with other creative hubs. Orlina Teo, a student at Nanyang Technological University, Singapore, was awarded such a grant in 2012. She has set out to create an assistive device to enhance mobility for the disabled, a way of expanding their horizons: "Watching someone transform through self-reliance and giving them confidence and happiness doubles my satisfaction", she says.

As well as spotting talent, Dyson intends to nurture it. Since 2008, the Foundation has run workshops at the Centre Georges Pompidou in Paris, encouraging thousands of young people to imagine what their house might be like in 2050, and what technology they would use. And in 2011, it launched the Engineering Lab at Science World in Vancouver, an exhibition and educational resource center. Its website says: "Children, with their natural curiosity are mini-engineers. They never stop to question, pulling mechanical (and sometimes expensive) things apart to get at the guts ... Let [them] find out for themselves just how rewarding design engineering can be."

CHALLENGE YOUR BRAND

- What tools can your brand offer to help someone on their journey?
- How can you support people to apply their own powers and skills in new ways?
- How will your brand become a guide throughout the adventure?

Brand navigation

We mark our journeys with milestones: building a cairn on a mountain, scratching "I woz ere" into a cliff face, placing a flag on the moon. There's a reward in seeing how far we have come, in marking a path for others to follow – or plotting our progress against the pioneers in whose steps we follow. Just as we need landmarks to help us establish where we are, so we need brands to help us find the resources we need and establish their value.

As Catarina Tagmark, Vice President for Corporate Brand and Design at Siemens, explains:

> Brands help us navigate in a more and more complex society. When you're out and about, you seek what you know. This is the fourth country I have lived in. One of the most stressful things [when you arrive

in a new place] is getting to that basic level of comfort in life. At these times, brands are helpful, because their symbols tend to pop out at you from the shelves; they are pointers that help you navigate.

Literal brand landmarks – such as the BT Tower in London or the Chrysler Building in New York – confirm this role. Brands can also help us to recognize people. We depend on trusted third parties to identify individuals who are reliable, or who have particular skills and resources to trade – through the educational and professional qualifications they confer, or the recommendation they offer in the form of prizes. This formalization of skills and qualities also prompts individuals to develop in ways that will be beneficial to society: skills as a team player, for instance, or knowledge of a particular industry. As accreditors and examination boards, brands have the potential to shape the development of a person's knowledge and skills in a very precise way. They can approach this as a leadership role, helping to hone the ability of individuals to meet the demands of society. Or, they can simply play to a sheer love of competition, inspiring people to push themselves further than they thought possible.

The rapid and unanticipated rise of the *Guinness Book of Records* to the top of the British bestsellers list within six months of publication is an indication of the potential for brands to inspire new adventures by recognizing and sharing successes. How many weird and wonderful contests have been organized simply to get a mention in this book! It was originally intended to be a marketing give-away but, over 50 years after it was first printed in 1954, it was itself recognized as a world record holder: the best-selling copyrighted series of all time. According to anecdote, the idea for it arose from an argument about the fastest game bird in Europe. In 1951, Sir Hugh Beaver – then Managing Director of the Guinness Breweries – had gone out shooting in County Wexford, near Dublin in Ireland, and got into an argument about whether it was the golden plover or the grouse. Neither answer was correct, but it struck Beaver that the regulars at pub quiz nights would welcome a collection of records to browse with their Guinness and solve their disputes.

Access to such trivia, over 60 years down the line, is transformed. Pubs have to ask quiz teams to turn off their smartphones to ensure they reward the team with the best general knowledge and not team Google. But with the rise in available data, the fascination in measuring ourselves and mapping our progress is also undergoing a shift. It's no longer just about updating a two-page curriculum vitae every year or two. More people are charting their day-to-day lives, and checking it against both their own past and the lives of their peers... How well did they sleep compared to last week? How much water did they use compared to next door? How fast do they walk compared to the average city-dweller?

The people asking these questions are moving from a more passive approach to their wellbeing – one led by impulse within certain parameters (for instance, "I feel like a snack and my choice depends on the content of the fridge") – to a much greater level of agency. Now, when faced with the urge to snack, some technophiles will pull out their phone and check the nutritional facts against their own records: "If I go for a biscuit, typically containing 80 calories and 10g of sugar, my blood sugar levels will rise a little and then take a dip, and after about 30 minutes I'll feel even more tired than I do now. Whereas..." – and so on. It's a trend known as self-tracking, or Quantified Self (QS), and app-builders are jumping at it.

As Gary Wolf, co-founder of the website QuantifiedSelf.com, recounts in the *New York Times*, this is precisely what Robin Barooah, a 38-year-old self-employed software designer who lives in Oakland, California, did to kick his coffee habit once and for all. Barooah had spent months weaning himself off it at a painstaking rate of 20 milliliters per cup per week. When, sometime after his last slim sip, he found himself tempted to have another cup, he wondered whether, although bad for his health, coffee was good for his concentration. As Wolf has it:

> Barooah wasn't about to try to answer a question like this with guesswork. He had a good data set that showed how many minutes he spent each day in focused work. With this, he could do an objective analysis. Barooah made a chart with dates on the bottom and his work time along the side. Running down the middle was a big black line labelled "Stopped drinking coffee". On the left side of the line, low spikes [indicating reduced concentration] and narrow columns [indicating shorter periods of concentration]. On the right side, high spikes and thick columns. The data had delivered their verdict, and coffee lost.[10]

Not every self-tracker has such a clear sense of purpose, however, says Wolf. Such quantification can simply be a journey of self-discovery, rather like keeping a diary. "Although they may take up tracking with a specific question in mind, they continue because they believe their numbers hold secrets that they can't afford to ignore, including answers to questions they have not yet thought to ask." Might a brand help them to uncover these inner secrets, and find questions to ask that could lead to a better quality of life?

Too close for comfort?

Few people would open their diaries to their friends, let alone a profit-making company. Life-logging data is arguably even more revealing. You can edit your experience for your diary entries if you like, and even if you were aiming for an honest record, your recollections are likely to be colored by your mood and how well your memory is trained. As Daniel Kahneman, winner of the Nobel Prize for his work on behavioral economics, argues, our memories can be markedly different to our lived experience. Data, on the other hand, is startlingly accurate. Tracking and analyzing a person's rhythms and reactions could offer a better insight into who they really are, and what they desire, than they could offer themselves. Which is why this is such a huge opportunity for brands. If they can prove they merit trust, they could move from the short-lived role of the likes of Q – providing gifts and gadgets to the adventurer before they set off – to the much longer-term role of the witty sidekick or faithful guide. The key is in the attitude of the brand towards people, the extent of its respect and the strength of its purpose. Will it use this intimate relationship to manipulate or to empower?

A service to help people collate their personal data and draw out its implications could enable them to approach life with much greater awareness of themselves. If they can take into account how all the various factors of their lives contribute to their wellbeing, or detract from it – their work and home, their friends and family, their location, how well they sleep, eat, exercise and so on – they may be able to make much wiser decisions about how they use their time and spend their money. The result could be a clearer path towards mental, physical and emotional wellbeing.

The market for centralized Quantified Self (QS) dashboards is already emerging, as Chris Hollindale, a self-tracker and co-founder of the healthy eating app Hasty, observes in the *Guardian*.[11] He describes the frustration of using one tracker to monitor his sleep, another for his weight, another for his exercise and yet another for his diet:

> This isn't ideal for a number of reasons. Firstly, it's difficult to view and evaluate all of the different tracked stats, as each service has a separate dashboard. It's difficult for me to find correlations between the different metrics – if I wanted to see the effect that my food consumption had on my weight over a period of time, I'd have to bring two different dashboards up and compare them manually.

He has spotted two trends that could solve the problem. One is multipurpose devices, such as FitBit and Jawbone, which allow you to track food intake, log your sleep and count your steps. At the moment these depend on manual entry, but Hollindale expects to see sensors in smartphones gather much more data in the future. The second trend is the dashboard, which can draw on data from a number of external apps and devices but "lets you view, compare and visualize your data in one place". TicTrac is one that he names. It allows you to "track almost anything … whether you want to lose weight, manage your time or watch your baby grow up" and it offers to help you "vizualize your data in the way that works best for you and discover what makes you tick". Its strapline? Know yourself.

A group of researchers and non-profit organizations have formed a movement called Transhumanism, which "favours [sic] allowing individuals wide personal choice over how they enable their lives". According to the Transhumanist Declaration, "this includes use of techniques that may be developed to assist memory, concentration, and mental energy; life extension therapies; reproductive choice technologies; cryonics procedures; and many other possible human modification and enhancement technologies". Peter Rothman, Editor of the associated magazine *Humanity+*, which aims to show how technology can enhance human existence, is optimistic about the potential. He imagines an app that would analyze bodily needs and the environment, drawing on real-time health data and environmental sensors, and then use predictive models to determine from an individual's wellbeing and circumstances what would meet their needs. For instance, it would identify "the actual nutritional needs of an individual before ordering food products and supplements".

Such a scientific approach to meeting needs could render marketing redundant, argues Rothman. Certainly, it could render approaches to marketing that treat the audience as passive consumers, as opposed to co-creators, redundant – as Philip Kotler argues in *Marketing 3.0*. Conversely, the risk for such an app would be a design that left people feeling as though their opinion wasn't sought or valued: they would soon lose interest. As Tagmark of Siemens asserts: "As a relatively well-informed consumer, I don't want to be told what I want, but I do want to be presented with things that make it easier to make a qualified decision." What such an app would do is mark out the brands whose products and services really do have a positive impact on wellbeing, and weed out the empty offers.

CHALLENGE YOUR BRAND

- How aware is your audience of the choices they make and their impact?
- How can you support people to learn more about their own needs?
- How readily do people share personal information with your brand?

Shared adventures

If community is one of your brand's core values, you might be inclined to dismiss the self-quantification movement as rather egocentric. Culture of Future's Jody Turner insists that it is not:

> It is all about tools that bring technology and people together in new ways, including deep metrics of community awareness. One of the attractions of novel technology for people is that they want to be part of evolution, they want to be involved. It can be a double-edged sword: they might simply want the latest gadget; on the other hand, they might be looking for ways to feel connected.

Turner points to the number of interactive technologies showcased at the 2013 South by Southwest (SXSW) Conference in Austin, Texas, to justify her point. SXSW isn't just a platform with an audience: it's all about interaction. The event grew out of the need for frustrated musicians "isolated from the rest of the world here in the middle of Texas" to reach out and connect with other creative professionals. As a brand, it exists to help people to relate their personal progress to the adventures of those around them, and come together with common goals.

The accusation of egocentrism could be levelled at almost any personal development pursuit. Take yoga, a practice that often takes place in silence, moved on by the soft sound of a gong: each person has their own mat, a space delineated for their own journey. Competition is not the essence: it's about you, your mind, your body and breath. So why does the Amrita Sanctuary for Yoga, in Portland, Oregon, put such emphasis on social interaction? Why did the studio decide, in 2009, that it "needed a way to build its community of students and connect with the greater yoga community"? Because research into the desires of its students found that they wanted to know each other better, and understand more about each other's progress, in order to remain engaged with their own practice and motivated to continue their journey.

Desire-led brands in action

This chapter began by asking how brands can respond to our desire to explore and discover, and through this to challenge ourselves and to develop as people.

We looked at the role of a brand as a storyteller, shaping aspirations by describing the journeys others have taken – as Dove did with the Real Beauty Sketches – and offering a platform for people to share their own tales with others.

We saw how brands can offer skills and tools to help someone get started on a journey – such as Caltech and the James Dyson Foundation – and considered how they can make the most of new digital platforms for learning. Then we asked how brands can help people navigate along the way, by offering familiar markers and supporting people to track their progress.

Presented below are three case studies to demonstrate how brands are developing their understanding of the desire for adventure by listening to their audience and responding to it. My hope is that, as you read these stories, the horizons of your own brand will grow.

For each one, we will consider how this brand illustrates the D – C – B – A approach, by asking:

* How does this brand learn about its audience's desire for adventure?
* How does it respond to this desire, and how does it involve its audience in its actions?
* How does this brand secure its place in new adventures?

Case studies

1 Nike+

Nike is well established as one of the world's largest and most highly recognized suppliers of sports shoes, clothing and equipment – the tools an athlete needs to get started on the road to physical power and prowess. But since 2006 it has been looking for ways to get much more involved in the adventure. In that year it collaborated with Apple to create an iPod device which used piezoelectric sensors (which generate electricity in response to applied mechanical stress) to measure the distance an athlete travelled, calculate their pace, log the time they spent doing sport, and count the calories they burned along the way. This was the beginning of Nike+. This sub-brand is more than just a QS device: it's a community of people pursuing goals and helping each other to find the best way forward. The website prompts people to sign up to "Stay motivated, challenged and connected". With Nike+, the brand shifts from its role as a provider of physical aids to the role of coach. For the athlete, it moves from a little "Swoosh" on their shoe to a companion for the journey. It's a much stronger proposition.

Nike+ offers to enhance an adventure in eight ways. It begins with helping you get to know yourself and your strengths better, by tracking multiple activities over time (running, walking, working out) and comparing your results. It can help expand your horizons by identifying new places to train and lets you plot new routes, or use those other people have taken. Then it offers support in setting goals and reaching them, with games and rewards to help you test your limits. Nike+ members can post their goals to this global community of athletes, or to their friends, by synchronizing the service with social media services Facebook, Twitter and Path – and they can use these platforms to set challenges for other people. Live stats on the website tell you that these members have taken over 65 billion steps and burned over 97 billion calories. The virtual community boasts access to professional coaches who can offer tips and advice, alongside analysis of new sporting lifestyle trends to help you keep up with the latest thinking on how to eat and when to rest.

Sports psychologist Dr Eva Monsma of the University of South California stresses the importance of setting short-term goals and charting them in order to progress. She says goals should be moderately difficult, measurable and preferably posted publicly: "Goals are ineffective if forgotten. Write them down, being as specific as possible. Keeping a journal or a publicly posted goal monitoring chart can help athletes and coaches with the monitoring process."

As we know, telling the tale is an important part of any adventure, and so Nike+ prompts runners to, "Describe how you felt, the weather, the terrain, the specific route you took. Even add a note to embellish the experience." Athletes are also prompted to share and celebrate their successes with the words, "There's no such thing as a small victory."

A recent jewel in the crown for Nike+ is the Fuelband, which was twice made available to order online before its official release in the shops and both times sold out on the same day. It looks like a very simple piece of kit: a little black wristband with an LED display and traffic light indicators so you can see your progress at a glance. Like the apps that came before it, it tracks your activities – each step taken and calorie burned. You wear it like a watch (it does also tell the time) but you can program it from your phone, and it will send visualizations of your progress back to your phone.

Demand for it was so high that the Fuelband was selling on eBay for double the retail price, after these initial web sales and before release in the shops. According to Nike's 2012 Annual Report, the company's performance in the fiscal year following the Fuelband's launch smashed its own records, with revenues growing 16 per cent and net income up 4 per cent. The report states that "the increase in revenues was driven by growth across all NIKE Brand geographies, key categories and product types", and attributes this growth to "brand strength" and "innovative products", with particular reference to the Fuelband.

What is behind the Fuelband's success? For one, there's the fact that you wear it. It marks you out as a recognizable member of a cutting-edge community, and a community of adventurers. It becomes part of your own style and identity, and yet links you with other people – both symbolically and through its virtual connectivity. Another attribute is that it offers this community an exclusive reference system, a new unit of measurement for tracking activity, known as NikeFuel. It means people can easily compare their progress even if they are training in different locations, are engaged in different activities, and have physical profiles that would mean they'd never compete in the same discipline on the ground. If you run through the key elements of an adventure story – an enabling gadget, a guide, a map, a community and new horizons – it ticks them all.

2 ASMALLWORLD

While Nike+ and many of the most influential social networks – from Facebook to music streamer Spotify to the room-letting platform Airbnb – cast their nets far and wide for as many members as their data servers can connect, ASMALLWORLD (ASW) is doing the opposite. This 21st century travellers' club connects jetsetters looking for exclusive experiences around the world. It was founded in 2004 as an invitation-only social network by Count Erik Wachtmeister – a digital enthusiast with an MBA from the leading European business school INSEAD. He garnered the support of American film producer Harvey Weinstein, co-founder of Miramax Films, at a time when social networks were still fairly niche. In 2009, the majority share was bought by the Swiss entrepreneur Patrick Liotard-Yogt, who became its Chairman. Before its re-launch in May 2013, the brand uninvited most of its members, including some fallen celebrities like Tiger Woods and Lindsay Lohan. Then it asked the somewhat tighter circle to pay for the right to remain. Who did this leave? The likes of Bibhu Mohapatra, a fashion designer in love with sumptuous fabrics and vibrant colors. The Grammy Award-winning violinist Joshua Bell. The party-loving DJ Chelsea Leyland. The jewelry designer Waris Ahluwalia, whose elaborate rings sold out at House of Waris. The model Tali Lennox, who describes herself as "a fruit of sorts, in search of the next adventure". And another 250,000 hand-picked "fruits", from every country in the world.

What did they pay for? Each other. That is, "a private international community of culturally influential people, connected by three degrees". They define the community that makes ASMALLWORLD an aspirational club through the relationships they build within it and the events they co-create. The brand offers them the freedom and infrastructure to do so, encouraging them to make ASMALLWORLD the epitome of their desire for an exclusive community of like-minded international travellers. Each one brings a personal perspective on locations across the world and support to experience them in ways far beyond the well-trodden paths of tourists. They venture into a realm where "members do adorable things for each other", the sort of thing a friend would do, such as filling the bride's side of a church for a wedding her relatives couldn't make, or finding the best doctor on demand and squeezing an appointment in ahead of any waiting list, or lending a "nowhere-to-be-found next-season smoking hot evening dress".

It's also a realm where ASW's corporate partners do "adorable things" for them, offering benefits from luxury spas to discounted stays in luxury hotels – including some of those in The Leading Hotels of the World (LHW) group – through the brand's Member Privileges Program. Even the ASW's advertisers come bearing gifts: they are required to do so as a post-selection process condition, earning them the opportunity to pay to place their offers within view of this privileged group.

It's a bold business model, but one with a strong rationale. For the Privilege Partners and advertisers, this is a highly targeted audience, and one whose appetite for rarity is heightened within this tightly defined context where all are keen to impress. "Walking around with a guidebook and looking at the Eiffel Tower doesn't seem like a modern way to travel", CEO Sabine Heller explains in *Harper's Bazaar*. "People want to be able to travel like insiders – and the only way to really do that is through meeting locals. Our members are able to tap into local communities wherever they go – they are never alone."

Heller has been CEO since August 2011 but has been involved from 2007, and was crucial to its restructure. She brings her experience, and presumably contacts, from a prior role heading up a boutique marketing practice whose clients included Gucci and Gilt Group. She has also led the corporate communications team of the digital entertainment platform UGO, where one of her award-winning marketing campaigns earned her a cover feature in the publication *Brandweek*.

Hers is the ideal profile to take the exclusive gentlemen's club of Victorian England and revamp it for the 21st century. In 1832, Charles Barry built a Pall Mall mansion to offer gentlemen who travelled abroad, their visitors and diplomats a privileged place to stay and to meet each other. ASW has no need of a Mall address: it has access to mansions, and their owners, all over the world. Other open networks, such as Twitter, Facebook and Pinterest, serve as its shop window. Its members talk openly to each other on these sites, and even post some of their videos and travel snaps. Many of the links are routed back to member-only pages on ASW, though, raising the curiosity of outsiders. The brand also publishes a public blog, The Globalist, which features road diaries, interviews with members, and travel features – and offers a peek into a series of City Guides.

The members themselves pay "a very affordable" rate to join: US $105/year, plus a mandatory $5 donation towards the ASMALLWORLD Foundation, which supports three carefully chosen non-profit charities to address issues in global health, education and women's rights. Their journey begins with the receipt of their pass, a card for their wallets that will open doors to them – rather like the introductory letter D'Artagnan received from his father – and new members have been known to tweet their delight. The membership card was designed by Waris Ahluwalia, the jewelry maker, who also features in a film by Jonathan Olinger that dominates the homepage of the public website. It shows Ahluwalia striding slowly and confidently always from right to left across the frame – through parks, snowy landscapes, past ancient ruins and wildflower meadows – in Europe, North Africa and the US, and even with a donkey in tow. Another film – less creative, more advertorial – describes the adventure-led life that ASMALLWORLD's members aspire to:

> We travel. We explore. We live boldly. We are a community on a journey that is defined by our experiences and the people we meet along the way. The farther we go, the more the world opens up to us, and possibilities become endless.

A promotional offer in The Globalist invites readers to apply to feature in *The ASW Adventurer*: a short film series in which two people travel to cities to which they have never been before, know no one, and have made no plans in advance. They are given three gifts "to kick-start their adventures": a limited budget, access to the ASW mobile app, where they can check in with other members and be offered local tips, and a party thrown by other members in the area. Janina Joffe, Director of the art and design collectors' platform East of Mayfair, featured in the trial run of the series: "I was not only invited into people's lives, but even their homes", she recounts. "I went from being dressed up as a geisha to attending a private Opening Ceremony party to singing karaoke at a hidden-away bar at 3am. I must have been the only tourist in a 3-mile radius."

Many travellers with an open mind, and likely an even more limited budget, are now meeting each other, sharing their homes and gaining local insights through the open-access online network Airbnb. I am writing this chapter from the home of the artists Timothy Maslen and Jennifer Mehra in the seaside town of St Leonard's on the East Sussex coast, having contacted them through Airbnb. For £34 a night and no membership fee, they have welcomed me in, taken me for a long walk along the seafront to Hastings, made me try the local shop's notorious sour bomb sweets, shown me a good vegan wifi café, pointed out the best pubs (and the ones to avoid), offered me a bowl of home-made muesli, seeds and nuts for breakfast, and shared with me their fresh mint brew from the garden. Few trips could be more gratifying in terms of gaining an insider's perspective.

And so what is the allure of ASW? For one, there is the feeling of trust inspired by a highly personalized service. Airbnb relies on consumer reviews, but there's an element of risk: you know very little about the people you will meet through this vast network. ASW offers the assurance of its very selective approach. It inspires each member to identify with the others, conferring their sense of personal worth on those that they meet. "I was chosen because I am special", runs the logic: "Therefore, if you were chosen, you too are special." Another draw is that these chosen ones are offered the opportunity to co-create a universe to themselves – rather like a child's den: they can set the rules, establish their own culture, and challenge what it means to travel, to be a tourist, to be, in Heller's words, "a citizen of the world". With each invitation, ASW offers someone the opportunity to become the hero of their own adventure story, in a world they can both explore and define.

3 Mulebar

Adventure isn't always something that the digestive system enjoys. While the mind is stimulated by street culture or mountain views, the belly is getting acquainted with unfamiliar bacteria or the impacts of altitude. When a couple of entrepreneurs, Alex and Jimmy, experienced this in the Andes, "pretty high up at about 6200m" on Cerro Aconcagua, they decided adventurers needed a better fuel. They set out to create something that would have little chance of getting in the way "when you're really out there", and yet be tasty enough to eat as an everyday snack. There's nothing particularly innovative about an energy bar, or gels and bites, as a concept, but the existing market for sports nutrition was heavily dependent on heavily processed artificial ingredients and additives. "The body has to work to process them and the more time the body is working in that way, the lower the performance level", they surmised, and set out to create high-energy nutrition from "real food".

Like many start-ups, Mulebar started out in a shed with its owners "skiving off the dayjob" and testing early prototypes on their biker and climber mates. They knew what they wanted themselves, but they needed to make sure it met the desires of other adventurers. Fortunately, "guinea pigs are easy to find when food's involved." A wider audience wasn't hard to find either: they would simply go to cycling and mountain-biking races with free samples and get feedback on the spot. "After about ten times of turning up to races and being told our bars were better than the ones on sale we thought we'd better do something about it."

They set up a company, Fuel for Adventure Ltd, and named the product Mulebar – inspired by one they had seen up in the Andes, with its obvious connotations of determination, endurance and strength in extreme habitats. The brand's language and character remains very informal: they started out as mates, not business partners, and they talk to their growing following in the same way – as Alex and Jimmy, without job titles or family names. They aim to use ingredients that are as easy on the planet as they are on the stomach, sourcing organic stock, certified by the Soil

Association, wherever possible. Mulebar is committed to buying Fairtrade stock as the ingredients become available, recognizing that good resource management depends on decent wages and a lifestyle to which the next generation of growers and producers can aspire. The products are sold in compostable packaging, a film made from wood pulp from sustainably managed forests (certified by the Forest Stewardship Council), which will biodegrade in eight to ten weeks in a home composting unit, or under six weeks in an industrial context. The idea is not to encourage climbers and cyclists to litter their surroundings but to mitigate damage if they do, and reduce waste to landfill.

It's a utilitarian approach to food: Mulebar's primary aim is to ensure people have the energy to enjoy exploring beautiful surroundings; the experience of consuming it comes second. The mission statement declares, "We are trying to help everybody get out on an adventure. We strongly believe that everybody's definition of adventure is different and that while some need to try and climb K2 or Everest or win the Tour de France, many just want to go for a ride or a walk at the weekend, go fishing or kick about on the local field." Nonetheless, they pride themselves on reviews that describe the products as "good enough to eat when you're not on your bike" – and this means they can include "sculptors, winemakers and dairy farmers (yes really)" among their adventurers, as well as Tour de France winners, World champion Ultraman racers, Ironman competitors and triathletes.

When developing the products, they brought in Matt Lovell, the nutritional advisor for the England Rugby Union, to help get the right balance of ingredients. For each bar, they make a point of educating adventurers about how to eat for the optimum impact on their performance. For instance, the MegaBites, made with glucose from organic brown rice syrup, fructose from natural fruit sugars and slower releasing sugars from oats and rice, are designed for easy consumption on the go. One or two should be consumed in the 30-60 minutes before event or training, and one to three per hour while you train. "Spacing carbohydrate out like this is more effective than having one large dose at the beginning and kinder to the stomach!" they explain, with a nod to their rather "unkind" experience in the Andes.

How does Mulebar encourage its adventurers to share their own stories? It has built up a team of ambassadors, which they call their "Mules", and describe as both "real characters who are passionate about what they do" and often winners who "are pushing the limits of their field". Among them is the professional mountain bike racer Petra Wiltshire, who has been a British National Downhill Champion, twice European Masters Downhill Champion, and three times Masters Downhill World Champion. She also teaches skiing in Switzerland. Her blog describes her adventures – "a few short climbs … wide open grassy sections … slippery off camber sections … the killer climb midway." She also makes a point of thanking the Mulebar duo: "These guys really rock and love life, riding and having fun", she says, directing her fans to their site.

Other Mules include an amateur women's cycling team called MuleBar Girls, also sponsored by Sigma Sport, whose aim is to inspire other women to get into cycling. This team organized a festival-style track racing day for women called Velo Jam, extending the brand's reach to 50 more women riders.

One cyclist keen to tell his story is the independent reviewer David Else. He describes his use of Mulebar gels on several four-hour training rides: "…they definitely work – giving enough energy to keep me cruising along for 30 to 60 minutes, depending who I'm trying to keep up with, before needing another one". He goes into the practicalities, including the shape of the sachet – a V-shaped notch which is easier to open with your teeth with one hand as you ride: "It also means a small hole, so the gel can be squeezed out in a controlled fashion, and you don't get it all over your hands. It also means the little tear-off bit stays attached to the main sachet so you can stuff the whole lot back in your pocket when finished and not litter the countryside." And he comes back to the very reason that got the two adventurers in the Andes thinking – a good indication that Mulebar has understood what adventurers really want: "As with other Mulebar products, all of the ingredients in these gels are natural, and the Soil Association logo on the packet indicates that most are organic. So if you find the compositions of some other gels give you stomach ache, then these Kicks would be well worth a try."[12]

Aesthetics

chapter **3**

Our senses are the interface between our mind and our immediate physical context. They serve many functions, helping us to navigate our way, find food and recognize dangers. The sweet smell of strawberries attracts us to a fruit, while the bluish tinge of rotting food alerts us to a threat. But the relationship between our senses and our wellbeing goes beyond mere survival: we enjoy the lavender plains of Provence without foraging through them, leaving the bees to enjoy the taste. Aesthetics describe this appreciation of the world through our senses, and the desire to find beauty in our surroundings.

Each of us responds to the world around us in a unique way. Our personal aesthetics are to some extent determined by our habits and by what we are exposed to. If you are accustomed to hearing low volumes and frequencies, you might find listening to a soprano with a shrill voice rather painful. As we grow and explore new sensory realms, our tastes develop too. Imagine going from bright sunlight into a dark room: you won't be able to see the colorful tiles on the wall, let alone appreciate their intricate patterns. But exposure isn't everything; our aesthetics change, sometimes – seemingly – of their own accord. "A man loves the meat in his youth that he cannot endure in his age", says Benedick in Shakespeare's *Much Ado About Nothing*, turning to the fickle nature of aesthetics to quash the embarrassment he feels at his own abrupt change of heart.[1]

While many factors could be called upon to explain our differences, it is perhaps more interesting – particularly for brands – to accept them. They offer a better starting point for one-on-one conversations than the broad brush of an acknowledged trend. Children often ask questions like "What's your favorite color?", building up simple character studies. One person might find beauty in a bleak moorland mist, another in soft evening light on a lawn. You might be tempted by a dish of smoked mackerel on sourdough, while your friend opts for steak and chips. As the idiom goes, there's no accounting for taste.

Everyday aesthetics

There's a difference between appreciating the material world and appropriating it. Critics of "affluenza" – the desire to amass ever more wealth and goods to "keep up with the Joneses" – have sometimes swept aside the material world altogether, as a result of the very valid argument that a greater focus on our values offers a more direct route to wellbeing. As the economist Tim Jackson demonstrates, there is a point (which he identifies as around $15,000 per capita) where the positive impact of economic growth and increased spending power on reported levels of happiness and satisfaction plateaus. He notes that "reported life satisfaction has remained more or less unchanged in most advanced economies over several decades in spite of significant economic growth".[2]

We get richer, but we don't get happier. Importantly, if we overdraw on the world's material resources, we also impinge on our future prospects of life – let alone life satisfaction. Stepping away from so-called "mindless materialism" is often caricatured as a step "back" to a simple lifestyle dismissively associated with cave dwellers. But a healthy approach to our material surroundings is not the same as a rejection of them. Quite the opposite: the more we value the material world, the more open we will be to any positive impact it can have on our wellbeing, and the better we will care for it in the long run.

Virginia Postrel, an American columnist specializing in commerce and culture, warns against too hasty a dismissal of aesthetics in her book *The Substance of Style*. "[R]ejecting our sensory natures has problems of its own. When we declare that mere surface cannot possibly have legitimate value, we deny human experience and ignore human behavior."[3] The essayist Alain de Botton, an Honorary Fellow of the Royal Institute of British Architects, also argues for the impact of our daily surroundings on our mental wellbeing to be taken more seriously. "A thought-provoking number of the world's most intelligent people have disdained any interest in decoration and design, equating contentment with discarnate and invisible matters instead", he observes in his book *The Architecture of Happiness*.[4] He recommends that we resist the "urge to override our sense and numb ourselves to our settings", and instead accept our susceptibility to our environment and take proactive measures to make it more pleasing, even if it "means conceding that we are inconveniently vulnerable to the color of our wallpaper…"

Of course, not everyone has the freedom to do so. You may not own a room, let alone the wallpaper. In the most challenging circumstances, numbing your senses to the world around you may be your best defence. However, the potential for our sensory experience to inflict such distress strengthens the case for giving them due consideration in design. This is not merely a concern for the wealthy. In Haiti, where 350,000 people are still living in temporary shelters following the 2010 earthquake, a collaboration of artists and engineers from the US has been working with local communities to design semi-permanent, disaster-resilient housing, using locally available materials, "in a way that acknowledges the importance of soulfulness and beauty in people's daily lives".[5]

Almost all civilizations have recognized this importance. Think of the spaces that have been designed with our spiritual lives in mind: the wide courtyards of mosques, the tall columns of cathedrals, the steps up to ancient temples perched among the clouds. The desire for surroundings that enhance our inner lives shows no sign of abating. Relatively recent additions include Brasilia's Catedral, dedicated in 1970, which one enters through a dark tunnel into a vibrant, light space beneath a stained-glass watery sky of blue, green and white; New Delhi's Baha'i temple, inaugurated in 1986, which emulates a large white lotus surrounded by water; Barcelona's Sagrada Familia, begun in 1882 and due for completion in 2026, where columns mimic natural woodland, defying any man-made grid, and The Sheikh Zayed Grand Mosque in Abu Dhabi, completed in 2007, where a unique night-time lighting system reflects the phases of the moon. Many of these designs invoke the natural world, suggesting a correlation between our sensory openness and our inner lives. Increasingly, architects and land planners are promoting green space in urban areas, recognizing the positive impacts of relaxing and exercising outdoors on mental health and reported quality of life, as well as the wider benefits of biodiversity and the potential for local food production. Think New York's High Line, or the wildflower meadows of London's Olympic Village...

CHALLENGE YOUR BRAND

- How sensitive is your audience to the particular qualities of their surroundings?

- How could your brand use everyday contexts to stimulate the senses?

- Which of the five senses is most important to the relationships you build as a brand?

Senses and sensibility

The technology specialist and TED Fellow Evgeny Morosov blames designers and marketers for paying too much attention to function and not enough to form. "The idea is that things deliver what you expect them to deliver and nothing else... We put far less stress on taste and the sensual experience that we get."[6] Morosov is concerned that we are in danger of side-lining aspects of our experience that are determined by quality. He refers in particular to the trend of self-quantification, which we observed in Chapter Two, and warns against a scenario in which "you look at a painting not to see what thoughts and feelings it triggers in you; you look at the painting because a key indicator in your life is running low and your Google Glass is telling you to look at a painting". It's not difficult to imagine a device so smart it can recommend you pick a Mark Rothko rather than a Jackson Pollock. And the painting may yet trigger your feelings.

Brands can use the impact of our surroundings on our wellbeing as an opportunity for engagement, asking people about their tastes, observing how they respond in particular contexts, and making recommendations. They might use a QS app as a tool, but they can build on the information it offers by using it as a springboard for personalization, tailoring their products and services through creative processes which involve their audience. They can even make this creative experience their primary proposition. Take the theatre company Punchdrunk. It has pioneered a form of presentation in which each member of its audience continually chooses their perspective on the action, through immersion in a theatrical setting which they are free to explore. In 2013, Punchdrunk staged *The Drowned Man* in a huge five-story warehouse in Paddington, London. One floor resembled the backstage rooms of a Broadway show, another a city street with food stores, toy shops and a cinema, and another created a woodland setting with caravans interspersed between the trees. The audience was free to follow the various performers as they moved through various sketches and choreographed scenes, or simply to be led by their own senses – from the strong scent of pot pourri in one room, to the sound of a jazz ensemble coming from another, or the bright lights of a cabaret show. Instead of the formal separation of stage and stalls, the audience members wore masks, which allow them to get as close as they wish to the action, and yet to feel it is going on in spite of their presence. "The audience is the camera floating around this dream", the Artistic Director Felix Barrett said. "All we are doing is presenting loads of content like the unedited rushes for them to cut together."[7]

Such exploration doesn't have to be confined to the dream-realm of theatre. The co-creation of home and work spaces, or even a family meal, could begin with an excursion into the unique sensibilities of individuals in its audience. How do they respond to each of their senses, and which elements matter most to them? It may never have occurred to them to question whether they find the darkness in their room oppressing, or whether listening to music in the morning would help them to start their day with a smile, and so they welcome the opportunity to think about its impact on their quality of life. The brand can then help to assess how well their environment matches their aesthetics, and work together towards solutions – playing out the human-centered design process advocated by IDEO that we touched upon in the Introduction.

Of course, an individual's surroundings may well be in flux, or beyond their immediate control: they may travel a lot; they may not own a property; they may not have the budget or confidence to rip out a wall or paint the floorboards. These inhibiting factors may well have led to a chronic sense of aesthetic disempowerment, to which they have responded by switching off their senses and burying their head in their hands. It might take a brand to gently raise their head, and help them to assume a more assertive attitude. Which aspects of their surroundings can they influence? What support do they need to take the first steps?

A question of confidence

This process of creative empowerment raises an interesting question: to what extent can we alter our perceptions of the world around us? A joint report by Forum for the Future and the consumer advocacy group Which?, asking how current trends might evolve to affect consumers in 2030, notes the effect of a widening income gap on the reported wellbeing of those living in the UK: "The percentage of people in the second-lowest income group who think that they are living comfortably, fell from 69 per cent in 2003 to 48 per cent in 2010", in contrast to the satisfaction levels of the highest-earning group, which fell by only six percentage points over the same period, to 82 per cent.[8] The authors project that the impact of this income gap will increase to 2030, as people in the lower income categories are disproportionately affected by food and fuel prices. As well as the economic question of relative spending power, the study raises the question of relative perceptions of comfort. The people surveyed weren't asked "Are you living comfortably?" but "Do you think you're living comfortably?"

The potential for brands to help individuals engage with their surroundings is clear, but there are two ways to make things better. One is to change the surroundings: the brand offers support in thinking about its qualities more carefully, and helps the individual to make it a better match for their aesthetics. The other option is to work with the person's perceptions: what is it that makes them feel satisfied with their surroundings? What other qualities are they not seeing? What is their benchmark?

This may sound somewhat manipulative: it's not meant to. The brand is not there to tell the person how to perceive anything; it is there to help the person realize they have a choice. As the Stoic philosopher Epictetus taught, "Man is disturbed not by things, but by the views he takes of them"[9]; or, as Hamlet says, "there is nothing either good or bad, but thinking makes it so". He recognizes that, while Denmark seems a prison to him, its confines are in his own mind.[10] Epictetus responded with acceptance of the world around him; Hamlet with resistance to it.

Brands can encourage people not to feel victims of their surroundings, instead taking charge of their response. We often assume that how we feel is the direct consequence of the world around us. "I feel oppressed because the ceiling is too low"; "I feel positive because the sun's shining", and so on. We talk about our desires in a similar way: "That cake smells delicious, I'd really like a slice". If you turn these thoughts around, the cake is appetizing because you associate its smell with positive experiences. People who see themselves as connoisseurs tend to take this second approach. They might say, "I have a particularly strong appreciation of the peaty scents of Islay malts, and so I'd like a glass of Laphroig". The implication is that their personal taste contributes as much to their enjoyment as the whisky itself. You don't have to be a connoisseur to take this stance: it's a question of confidence. You can choose, like a Stoic, to accept your surroundings. You can choose, like Hamlet (in one interpretation of that exceedingly complex play, at least!), to be its victim. Or you can choose, like a connoisseur, to beautify them.

Brands can support people to become wizards at beautification, first by increasing their confidence as judges of their own experiences, developing their sense of what they like and why, and then guiding them to make better choices.

CHALLENGE YOUR BRAND

- How could your brand support people to be more assertive about their tastes?
- In what ways could your brand work with people to create experiences tailored to their aesthetics?
- How could you help your audience to experience familiar surroundings in new ways?

Why be comfortable when you can be challenged?

The Forum for the Future/Which? survey asked people whether they thought they were living comfortably. But comfort isn't the only positive experience our surroundings can offer. Brands could start a much more interesting conversation about lifestyle aspirations by asking not whether people think they are comfortable, but whether comfort is what they're after in the first place. What do they want from their homes, holidays, working space or clothes? For any hardened camper ("glampers" are the exception), comfort is low on the list. Price might come top. But they might also appreciate the challenge of pitching a tent and warding off creepy crawlies, and the contrast to home furnishings. They might be looking for peace and quiet, and find it on the edge of a meadow with a view of the stars. Or perhaps they just love the smell of smoke from a campfire.

Vincent Stanley, Vice President of Marketing at the outdoor clothing brand Patagonia, rejects the emphasis on comfort in consumer culture, which he believes "tends to dull the mind".[11]

> I think it's a problem… I think we're too comfortable. The opposite of comfort isn't distress. We all know we feel better if we exercise. We know we feel better if we use our talents, if we engage. I think there's an ideal of comfort as a kind of disengaged state of relaxation and an absence of problems, a sort of control over your life by lack of involvement with anyone else. This is a kind of retreat state that everybody has been attracted to, probably because of the rough and tumble way that we live, to get out of the rough and tumble of the city to the isolation of the suburb. I think we have to get away from the idea of comfort as a kind of goal for ourselves. I think engagement, with some pitched moments of relaxation – which is a normal way of living – has to be our goal.[12]

Time in the wilderness can help people to see beyond the desire for comfort, opening up their senses to a much wider spectrum of experience. Even though we may feel less secure than we do in a closed environment, being outdoors can help to dismantle our need to feel in control. Studies show that active time outdoors can decrease stress, anger, confusion and depression, and enhance mood and self-esteem.[13] Some of these studies point to the contrast between indoor distractions – in particular the prevalence of screens and software, and their constant demands on our attention – and the relative stillness of the natural world. Its life moves at a slower pace: the tree won't go into standby mode if you don't pay attention to it;

Comfort isn't the only positive experience our surroundings can offer

you don't need to prompt the squirrels to run across your path. You can simply be there, and the world will carry on too. Your life comes into a new perspective: you are smaller than the tree and younger, taller than the sapling but it will outlive you. You scramble up the rocks and note the comparative agility of the goats, or the tenacity of the tiny purple flower in the crevice as your fingers search for a hold. Perhaps this release from our self-centered anxieties is what we are really looking for when we sit down in a comfy chair.

While the outdoor world can offer our senses a particularly engaging experience, there's no reason why our indoor environments shouldn't do so, too. Stanley wants people to associate their experience of Patagonia with the stimulus of being in the great outdoors. "When someone walks into our store, I want them to feel a little bit of relief from the street. I want them to feel that on the website too", he says. You log on and find yourself gazing into a crevice with someone hanging off a cliff-face; scroll to the next shot and someone is plunging into a cool mountain pool; click play and you can almost imagine you're out surfing in the South Pacific.

There's rising interest among architects and designers in ways to make our urban environments less comfortable and more stimulating. The pioneers include the Japanese architect Shusaku Arakawa (1936–2010) and his wife, the American artist, poet and architect Madeline Gins. This couple built the Bioscleave House in Long Island, New York, where undulating, textured floors, curiously shaped rooms on various levels, windows where you wouldn't expect them and hard-to-reach light switches aim to keep residents on their toes, and an absence of doors forbids the sense of closed privacy. Comfort, these designers claimed, is a precursor to death. Their designs aimed to help people remain young, by keeping their senses engaged and their minds open to awe and wonder.[14]

Their work inspired the architect Philip Beesley and scientist Rachel Armstrong to create Hylozoic Ground, an installation first displayed at the Venice Architecture Biennale in 2010. This immersive space feels like a jungle of hanging vines, creepers, fronds and whiskers, which respond to the presence of visitors by convulsing, breathing out air, caressing passers-by and changing color. The name refers to "hylozoism", the notion that all matter is alive, from the Greek *hyle*, for "matter", and *zoe* for "life". The whole space mimics the sensory responses of a body, thanks to an embedded "neural network" – a range of sensors which are affected by the temperature and chemical presence of humans, and by variations in airflow caused by their movements.

There is something attractive about an environment that recognizes and responds to us – rather like the exaggerated sense of your own presence you feel if you find yourself face to face with a fox or a deer and it stares back at you. Many authors and poets explore these encounters with wild animals, but some also refer to our inanimate surroundings as though they are alive and have their own perspective; the effect tends to be more nostalgic than spooky. The philosopher Gaston Bachelard – whose volume *The Poetics of Space* discussed "setting" as a much more active force in our lives than a backdrop – observes that "a rather large dossier of literary documentation on the poetry of houses could be studied from the single angle of the lamp that glows in the window... The lamp keeps vigil, therefore it is vigilant. And the narrower the ray of light, the more penetrating its vigilance."[15] Virginia Woolf illustrates this with a description of the stroke of a lighthouse passing through a room – "as if it laid its caress and lingered stealthily and looked and came lovingly again".[16]

If art and literature can prompt us to recognize and appreciate the role that our surroundings play in our lives, it may not feel such a leap from innovations like the Bioscleave House and Hylozoic Ground to the creation of more interactive, stimulating environments in the mainstream. It's already common for sensor-enabled lights to respond to our movements; could they soon respond to our mood? Imagine LEDs performing a little dance on your wall, with the message "Lighten up!"...

CHALLENGE YOUR BRAND

- If your brand could write on the wall in LED lights, what would it say?
- Is your audience seeking comfort, stimulus or exhilaration? Sofa, campsite or cliff face?
- If your brand built a house, what would it feel like to live in?

Aesthetics in a hyper-connected world

A very significant technological shift means that our surroundings are moving towards hyper-connectivity, whether we like it or not, and more rapidly than many of us are aware. Some propose the emergence of a super intelligence through artificial means – a "technological singularity" – which would have an overview of human systems and affairs. Already, more objects are now connected to the internet than there are people on the planet. Cisco's Internet Business Solutions Group (ISBG) is keeping track with a live connections counter, which showed that, in July 2013, the number of people, processes, data and things connected to the Internet at any one time exceeded 10 billion. The ISBG expects 50 billion devices to be connected by 2020.[17] This phenomenon is known as the Internet of Things (IoT), referring to ubiquitous sensors which connect everything in the physical world to our ever-expanding digital realm. This term was first proposed by Kevin Ashton, while working in supply chain management at Proctor and Gamble. He was engaged in the process of linking the company's vast range of consumer goods to the internet using radio frequency identification (RFID) when he had an idea: "If we had computers that knew everything there was to know about things—using data they gathered without any help from us—we would be able to track and count everything, and greatly reduce waste, loss and cost. We would know when things needed replacing, repairing or recalling, and whether they were fresh or past their best."[18] He went on to become the co-founder and former Executive Director of the Auto-ID Center at the Massachusetts Institute of Technology.

Since then, many more researchers, designers and brand strategists have become convinced by the potential. In 2010, three senior members of McKinsey imagined a world in which:

> Pill-shaped microcameras already traverse the human digestive tract and send back thousands of images to pinpoint sources of illness. Precision farming equipment with wireless links to data collected from remote satellites and ground sensors can take into account crop conditions and adjust the way each individual part of a field is farmed—for instance, by spreading extra fertilizer on areas that need more nutrients. Billboards in Japan peer back at passers-by, assessing how they fit consumer profiles, and instantly change displayed messages based on those assessments.[19]

The applications are limitless. Far beyond a building with its own nervous system, we are talking about a central system linking the whole world – "from jumbo jets to sewing needles", in the words of Helen Duce, President Asia at EffectiveBrands and former Director of the University of Cambridge's Auto-ID Centre. "Compelling as this vision is," she argues, "it is only achievable if this system is adopted by everyone everywhere. Success will be nothing less than global adoption."[20]

If this sounds a little ominous, it points to the need for trusted bodies to help manage the relationship between people and technology. The potential to maximize the benefits of connectivity, through more efficient systems, for example, depends on approaches to development that do not erode our willingness to comply with the common systems on which societies depend – from food to healthcare to energy. Brands can help with this, particularly if their operations are transparent and their communications clear and informative. They can also help to make radical changes more appealing and desirable. One approach would be to draw out the aesthetic possibilities of connectivity. For one, smart environments could anticipate our desires for a softer light, a cooler room, a brighter wallpaper, and so on – and respond to enhance our wellbeing.

This raises an interesting question: what is the likely impact of digital technology on our aesthetics – on our sensory awareness and appreciation of the world around us? What difference will Google Glass make? Instead of repapering the wall in reality, will we simply be content to impose a digital "wash", rather like rose-tinted spectacles? Such an innovation could radically disrupt the market for paint, and put a quick end to many household disagreements... In the first chapter, we touched on the impact of omnipresent media on our relationships with each other. Might greater connectivity have a similar impact on our relationships with our surroundings, numbing our sensitivities as opposed to enhancing our potential to make life beautiful? Already, when we venture into the wilderness, we interrupt our sensory interface with headphones, the voice of Runkeeper and unlimited tracks. Is there a risk that the more our digitally enhanced physical environment responds to us, the less we will respond to it?

Not necessarily, says James Bridle, author of "The New Aesthetic", a blog exploring the "eruption of the digital into the physical". He acknowledges that our perception of our physical surroundings, and the way in which we interact with them, is already influenced by digital technology – from satellite and pixelated imagery to mobile applications. But, he says, there is no reason why this should diminish our sensory appreciation of the world, or our ability to find beauty in it. In a keynote speech delivered at Web Directions South 2011, an annual conference in Sydney, he spoke of the "extraordinary beauty" he finds in the way in which people respond to the digital world – for example, in the gestures they make with their fingers, hands and arms as they use touchscreens. He points to the work of the artist Evan Roth, who has made a series of paintings based on these gestures.[21]

As brands explore their role in enhancing aesthetics, they should keep track of rising trends in hyper connectivity. It means bringing their audience's smartphone or augmented reality glasses into the room too, and seeing how it colors the conversation. There's no point painting a wall, if a new enhanced perspective can override hours of labor in a blink of an eye…

CHALLENGE YOUR BRAND

- How could your brand make use of the Internet of Things to enrich sensory experiences?
- How engaged is your audience in digital trends?
- How might your audience's aesthetics change in a hyper-connected world?

Decentralized design

Alongside this growing potential for digitally enhanced surroundings to play a more active role in people's lives, there are also more and more opportunities for people to reimagine and rework their own environments – and a greater appetite to do so. The IKEA Hackers blog and app is one example, with multiple posts each day showing how people from all over the world have reworked IKEA products to suit their needs, mixing and matching different parts, adding embellishments from other sources, or going to it with a power tool to make more radical changes. One post, from Oldenburg in Germany, offers a new shoe storage solution, using simple frames from IKEA, neon spray paint and planks taken from old wooden cases. Another, from Thessaloniki in Greece, shows a kitchen top transformed into a coffee table using four document storage boxes "beefed up" with carriage bolts as table legs. "So far, it seems to be sturdy enough", the hacker notes.[22] It's no bad thing for Ikea, potentially bringing more people into its stores in search of the necessary parts.

This DIY trend is partly fuelled by economic constraints: as spending power is squeezed by slow growth, lack of jobs and government cuts, people are looking for more creative ways to enhance their lives, drawing on resources to hand and finding multiple uses for them. But it has also become a trendy thing to do, showing off your carpentry skills to your mates, as opposed to your cash. There's also just the sense that, partly thanks to new technology and tried-and-tested models to get you started, you can come up with solutions yourself that will likely prove a better fit than the ready-made varieties in the shops. Craft skills are reviving too, with more cafes offering activity afternoons where you can knit new clothes or patch and darn old ones.

At the more high-tech end of the spectrum, ICT enthusiasts and entrepreneurs are coming together in hackathons – where they generate, prototype, test and refine new commercial ideas and solutions to civic problems in a very short space of time, pooling their tools and skills.[23] Manufacturing hubs are mushrooming outside of large, isolated FMCG factories, with the rise of 3D printing and local fabrication laboratories, or fab labs. In Hawaii, a DIY community has set up a space in a shipping container on the island of Maui, providing "tools, space, instruction and community to support the making of things".[24] In Tokyo's Shubiya shopping district, the FabCafé offers you the chance to make "everything from iPhone covers, greeting cards, accessories, chairs, lighting to even homes" while you have your coffee, thanks to a laser-cutting service.[25] And the desktop 3D printer manufacturer MakerBot was bought in June 2013 by the industrial company Stratasys for over $400 million, having sold more than 22,000 printers since it was founded in 2009.[26]

As people realize that they can create their environment, as opposed to merely consuming it, they are looking for a more engaged relationship with brands – one that recognizes their creative potential and offers them new outlets for it. According to a report by the New York-based brand innovation studio BBMG, two-thirds (67 per cent) of consumers globally are "interested in sharing their ideas, opinions and experiences with companies to help them develop better products or create new solutions".[27] As people take a more "hands-on" approach to how they spend their money, brands will need to respond with one that is more "hands-off".

Rachel Armstrong – the co-creator of Hylozoic Ground and a director of the virtual technology research group AVATAR at Greenwich University – sees an opportunity for brands in design approaches that leave more room for the *possible* and the *probable*, and are less constrained by the *actual*. Brands need to find ways *not* to offer a complete solution, but to explore and develop a response in collaboration with the people it will touch. The crowd-funding site Kickstarter offers start-ups a way to do this, sharing a prototype that can be developed if an audience comes forward with funding, and offering them the chance to give feedback before the design is finalized. The more people are involved in this early concept phase, the more likely they are to accept radical innovation within it, giving brands a greater space for experimentation. "The space of possibility is always greater than the event", Armstrong says, and so the most adaptable designs allow for multiple possibilities, offering more choice to users, so that they can also come up with innovative applications.[28] This way, the outcome will have greater meaning for them, and they will be more likely to accept any difference it makes to their current way of life.

For an example, Armstrong points to IBM's Smarter Cities Challenge, in which the technology company's experts work closely with city leaders for a three-week period, developing recommendations to make the city more effective, which are then explored and implemented over three years. "The most successful way of building the future is getting other people to use it", observes Armstrong. "IBM is providing tools and infrastructure, but these are secondary to their main proposition, which is a vision of cities and citizenship that others can share." She adds that creating visions is "much more exciting" than designing products. Unless, of course, you're in a maker space, doing it yourself...

CHALLENGE YOUR BRAND

- How can your brand create more space for possibility in its solutions?
- What creative talents might your audience have, and how can you harness them?
- Does your audience embrace change in their surroundings, or fear it?

Connecting to craft

As creative "prosumerism" grows, people are also expressing more interest in goods with their own stories to tell. It's not a counter trend. What makes a product interesting is its story: where it came from, who made it, how it travelled. These questions are easily answered if you just 3D-printed it – but the process of actually making something yourself is likely to increase your interest in how other objects come into being. There are other factors too: a rising awareness of the human impact of cheap production, with horror stories such as the collapse of the clothing factory in Dhaka, Bangladesh, in 2013, killing more than 1100 people.

The same year, India's Export Promotion Council for Handicrafts reported a 13 per cent surge in exports of hand-printed textiles and scarves, compared to the year before, owing to a revival in demand from the US market, and also to new orders from markets in Latin America, Africa and China.[29] Similarly, Bali reported that the value of exports of bamboo crafts by small enterprises increased by 22.8 per cent in 2012 on the previous year. Interestingly, the volume of exports had actually fallen, suggesting that foreign buyers were now assigning a greater value to the crafts.[30]

Both consumer trends – the creative impulse, and the interest in handicraft – are about connecting people to the world around them. As Barbara Coignet, Founder of the 1.618 Sustainable Luxury Fair, held every year in Paris, observes, "It's about the emotional charge of something that is going to last: its quality, the time it has taken to make, the know-how of those who made it..."[31]

The desirability of an object is certainly enhanced by its story, but to what extent does our knowledge of its past influence our aesthetic experience of it? Students of the arts mull this question over year after year, asking themselves whether they like a work more – or perhaps less – for having studied the composition process or read up on the artist's life. It's difficult to argue that it makes no difference: our minds are so quick to relate a sensory impression to a memory. As Proust famously described, we can travel from the taste of a cake to a childhood scene in a split second.

For Adam Lowry, co-founder of the US home cleaning company Method, aesthetics are very much a combination of sensory experience and the desire to celebrate people and community. Our long-standing cultural appreciation of our natural surroundings plays out in all our aesthetic experiences, he argues: "The human desire for beautiful things began with our appreciation of nature combined with the impulse to create things for ornamentation or ceremony. Those things became the totems of culture."

A strong cultural narrative, connecting people to the lives and values of other communities, combined with aesthetic appeal, makes for a very powerful proposition.

> There's a wheat flour brand called Stone Buhr Flour that you can use to bake cookies. Stone Buhr has created a bar code on the pack so you can trace it back to where your wheat was grown, and it'll show you the farmers that grew the wheat and where they are in Washington or Eastern Idaho or wherever it was... This creates a human connection for something that was simply a purchase at a grocery store, so that you can make cookies for your kids. That connectivity is incredibly important.

Lowry has a horror of pure functionalism without aesthetics – and, equally, of aesthetics without function. He set up Method to prove that:

> [Y]ou don't have to choose between ugly brown products that don't work and cost too much, and beautiful things that pillage the earth and burn your lungs. We aim to create the fragrance that just wows you and makes you say, "I'd love to have that in my bathroom" – or the beautifully designed bottle in the shape of a teardrop that you just have to have on your counter-top. These things taken by themselves could be superficial, but combined with a product that has been thought through from source to use to recycling, they are incredibly powerful.[32]

As Lowry sees it, the story behind the object is central to the aesthetic experience it can offer – whether or not the user is aware of it. The beauty of the bottle is very much the function of the fact the plastic is made from post-consumer recycled waste; the strong, sweet scent as you wash your hands depends on the health of the resources which nourish its ingredients. While an end-user may not be interested in the details of a product's lifecycle, they could make all the difference to a co-creator.

Desire-led brands in action

As we have seen, aesthetics is one of the most personal realms a brand can explore, with opportunities to ask its audience very intimate questions about their preferences, and learn about their personalities. A brand can support people to explore their senses – although this doesn't necessarily need to be through such radically immersive contexts as the sets of theatre company Punchdrunk or New York's Bioscleave House. Rather, they can take a page from Patagonia's catalog, and inspire people to head outdoors. Another role for brands is to encourage people to assert their tastes more strongly, developing the confidence of the connoisseur. Then, the brand can work with them to co-create new aesthetic experiences and shape their surroundings. They can enrich these experiences with stories, connecting people to the history of a product, the skills and culture of those who produced it, or its origins.

- These three brands each show the importance of the D – C – B – A approach to brand strategy: their success depends on understanding what people want to experience aesthetically, and how this relates to their cultural context, enabling the brand to respond in subtle, innovative ways. The key questions to bear in mind are: How has this brand learned about its audience's tastes and its members' desire for aesthetic experiences?
- How is it working with people to develop new stimuli for the senses?
- How does it respond to the very personal nature of aesthetics, but also to the cultural context?

Case studies

1 Wrap Art & Design

Furniture is a very recent industry in India, explains Gunjan Gupta, founder of the award-winning Indian interior and spatial design company Wrap.[33] It was introduced only 400 years ago when European settlers arrived, bringing with them the concept of elevated seating and so creating a need for chairs and tables. Before then, ground-based textiles were used for seating for meals, work and leisure, and the only raised surfaces were for storage chests and the like. The exception was the throne, and the brand's name gives a little nod to this: "wrap" is an ancient Indian throne decoration technique, referring to the use of pure silver sheets to coat the seat's frame. Wrap's contemporary thrones have attracted international design enthusiasts at the Milan Furniture Fair and the online gallery L'ArcoBaleno. One offers a seat made up of six cushioned bicycle saddles arranged in a star, with a back rest of silken quilt "bales" – inspired by the familiar sight of people pedalling around India with all sorts of bulky wares strapped to their bikes. Another of its thrones is a three-legged stool, common in India, wrapped in 24-carat gold and silver leaf. Both design concepts reinterpret contemporary design by incorporating Indian tradition and culture – and this, explains Gupta, is Wrap's unique selling point. It is an approach valued not only by European galleries with an intellectual interest in provenance and stories, but by Wrap's primary audience: the Indian upper class looking to distinguish their home or working environment. Gupta describes them as "a very special client with a lot of resources and a strong desire to be one-up on anyone in society; a wealthy client who is looking for something very off-beat. They come to Wrap, and we are able to translate their history into a contemporary lifestyle."

I ask her to explain how she and her design team goes about this.

We do not have a cookie cutter approach to interior design projects. It's a very customized approach, and this means taking the client's own tastes, history, background, experiences. So, we start afresh. Very honestly, it's a blank slate most of the time, and it's very challenging. The concept phase is broken up into several meetings where we get to know the client. In India we have old families, old traditional families with a very strong past that brings them from the villages into the urban centers of the country. As a result, they're carrying with them huge heirlooms of craft and textiles. As a company, we believe in incorporating and integrating these into a contemporary story, rather than imposing a contemporary or a modern, international perspective onto the client. It really is bringing their story to the forefront of the design process. I will give you a small example. One of my clients has this collection of jade and onyx figurines of traditional gods and goddesses, which has been in their family for the past hundred years or so. We are looking at these objects and asking how to bring them in. Instead of putting them into a traditional vitrine or showcasing them in ways that they would have been in the past, we are creating a sculptural chandelier out of them. We feel there is a lot of value in them; my client's family has collected them over a number of years.

Gupta contrasts this to the "looks" and trends in interior design that you might see at Milan's international fair. She explains that Wrap doesn't promote or patronize such currents at all; her ambition is to help her clients re-establish their own aesthetic identity, supporting them to break free of what she calls India's "copyist" culture:

> In India, interior design trends are strongly influenced by the West. It's a question of independence. India gained independence in 1947, but over 300 years it was hugely influenced and pride in Indian culture was affected by European settlers and British rule. It really changed our perspective on lifestyle. A different way of living has completely taken over, and as a result I don't think there is an identity in design in India. [Consequently,] you rarely ever plunge into a creative process: it's always the tried and the tested. You will pull up a catalog, or a magazine, and say "This is the look that I want". The majority of interiors follow an existing trend or an existing look to the "T". We are trying to challenge that whole perspective; we try to engage with a client and bring them into a creative process, so that the client is as much part of that process as we are.

For thousands of years before the arrival of European home furnishings, the aesthetics of space and interior design in India was dominated by the Hindi science of construction, *vāstu śāstra*, attributed to the great ascetic Maamuni Mayan, said to have lived in the period of the Ramayana, some 16,000 years ago.[34] One renowned Indian architect and Sanskrit scholar refers to his teachings as "a science of time and space, sound and light, word and form"[35]; another calls it "the science of energy that creates a rhythm and balance in the building to ensure a better quality of life"[36]; Gupta herself describes it to me as India's *Feng Shui*. When Wrap won a commission to transform an outdated farmhouse into a contemporary luxury dwelling, it looked for ways to bring the traditional [*vāstu*] framework into the design process, using it to enhance the aesthetic.[37]

"It's a very restrictive system", Gupta admits. "Quite often one finds that architects and interior decorators are at loggerheads with their client over this format of understanding. We just believe that this is part of the client's culture, and if this is what they want to incorporate then we have found ways and means of making it aesthetically more appealing."

The framework specifies how doors, windows, beams and columns should be spaced to enhance their impact on the senses, breath and energy of inhabitants. One contemporary interpretation, which extends to furniture, electricals and other mobile decor, notes that heavy furniture should be placed in the south-west, where the strength of the property lies, and light indoor plants can be placed in the north-east, the realm of purity. In consideration of these principles, Wrap kept the existing structure of the farmhouse, but added a canopy of stone and wood supported by copper columns to bring it in line with contemporary design trends.

Inside, the team used traditional design elements from across India: frescoes from Shekhawati in northern Rajasthan, inlays of polished colored stones in the style of Agra's *pietra dura*, *varksaaz* gilding from Jaipur, and traditional soft furnishings from Gota in Gujarat.

> Most entrances must have an idol, or a framed picture of a god; we found ways to make these elements far more interesting and unusual. For example, in the farmhouse, the foyer has hand-painted murals by an artist from Rajasthan in collaboration with a New York-based artist. We played with the iconography of the traditional entrance but did something completely different with it. It's still very welcoming, it's very auspicious; culturally, it's very much in line.

At the heart of Gupta's design principle, upon which she has established Wrap's character and reputation, is the belief that everyone has their own aesthetic.

> If you are able to get to that, if you're able to define that for yourself, or for someone else – and that's the critical point for me – it makes you feel very proud, and it's something that has longevity. This is design for posterity, for the future, it's for future generations. It's not a trend.

She contrasts India's "copyist culture" to what she sees as the main problem of the West: easy access, with constantly shifting trends. She observes a shift away from this disposable culture – "because it's been two decades of the same thing" – and because of rising awareness of sustainability among designers in the West. In India, the whole market for furniture and design is still nascent. There is almost no retail market for furniture in India, she explains, no equivalent of Ikea. The custom is for each family to have their own carpenter who they would call upon, in the same way that they have a family jeweler or tailor. This person will know your home, your taste and your requirements inside out. And so, for a commercial designer, personalization is crucial to success – but also a distinguishing factor, something to justify the effort of looking further afield.

"The aspect that concerns my client most when commissioning something from me is how highly customized it can be, how one-off it can be, how the objects can be perfectly tailored to their environment", Gupta explains. Her conversations with clients begin with her design process and how her designs can both be integrated into their space and also fit with their tastes. "A lot of my clients are buying...international design pieces, collectors' items from all over the world", she observes, and so her pieces must be a good fit with global trends and yet bring out India's traditions and cultural narratives.

Wrap's second market is international retailers and galleries. They are looking for a brand they can trust to be both a discerning eye and a professional project manager. Wrap offers to act as an interface between India's craft sector, which Gupta readily describes as highly disorganized and resistant to deadlines – though evidently with skills to make its outputs worth the wait – and the commercial export market, which relies upon predictable quality standards and tight schedules. "There's a huge difference in understanding between the production values that the designer brings in to a conversation with the craft people", she remarks – and the ability to bridge this is the strength of her brand. Wrap does it through a combination of long-standing relationships – working with some artisans in Rajasthan since 2006 – but also through new technology, such as 3D visuals, to help them see exactly what her client is looking for.[38]

Gupta once declared that her aim was to redefine the label "Made in India", and she has won recognition in international design magazines and at trade shows for doing so – with shows at the British fine art institute Sotheby's, Fuorisalone del Mobile in Milan, and Design Days in Dubai, design commissions with Droog Design in Amsterdam and Swarovski in

Paris. She was also named Designer of the Year at ELLE Deco International Design Awards 2012. She would like to see "Made in India" become a concept to which the country's next generation of craftspeople and designers can aspire, and hopes to influence other, more mainstream, design companies in this direction, shifting notions of India's vast manufacturing capacity away from cheap goods towards its rich cultural and artisanal heritage.

> Everyone has a certain vision of India, or a version of India. And this is not only true of India, but if you're travelling to the Middle East, or travelling to Europe. I think everyone has a certain "connect" with a culture. We aim to package that connect, whether it is through material, through story, we put that forward; that is the aesthetic that I think has been appreciated in what we do.

I ask her how she "connects" with India: what is her personal vision?

> Culturally, we have such a unique material palette. I have always been fascinated by the high and the low possibilities – right from pure gold or pure silver sheets that we use for wrapping to the semi-precious engravings or inlaid walls, to a whole range of other craft techniques. There is a local street culture which actually recycles a lot of found objects, a lot of metal, a lot of bicycle parts, and so on. Jute is an essential hand-woven Indian textile; it is really a poor man's cloth, but it's a material so beautiful and different from anywhere in the world that it has formed a very strong part of my vocabulary. The minute you wrap something in jute, it is so strongly Indian. To me, material and narrative are very interestingly linked.

2 Quantum Designs

Take an evening stroll through Paris, perhaps along the Rue des Abbesses in the lap of Montmartre, past the fruit sellers and caves à vin, or slip from the bustle of Bastille into the slim streets of the Marais, and you'll be sure to find people sitting out *en terrasses* enjoying a good *cassoulet* or a *boeuf bourginon* with a good bottle of CÔtes du RhÔne, and followed – almost impatiently – by an obligatory coffee (usually an espresso), a square of dark chocolate, and a cigarette. It's a ritual end to the meal: an invigorating sip and a long slow inhalation. It's a tradition only slightly knocked by the national ban on smoking in cafés. "What's the alternative?" Monsieur asks with a shrug, perhaps fearing the awkward pause it would leave in the conversation, the hindered escape from a highfalutin debate...

But the French-American Harvard scientist David Edwards thinks he has found an even more appetizing answer. What people want, he observes, is just the right combination of sensory stimulus and a treasured socio-cultural habit. He invented a novel way to offer it: aerosol chocolate that you draw through your lips, just as you might smoke a cigarette or drink from a straw. "Breathable" chocolate is now part of a line of AeroDesign products, including energy shots of caffeine and B vitamins.

Edwards has set up the company Quantum Designs to offer "trans-formative nutrition delivery" through "innovative products that broaden food experiences and enhance human health with minimal impact to the natural environment". In his book *The Lab: Creativity and Culture* he describes the reaction to an early prototype at a reception to which several hundred guests were invited: "Our guests had a ball with it. They invariably held it between their fingers as if it were a cigarette, and kept it long after the tube was empty, chatting, appreciating a novel social experience."

AeroDesigns uses the after-dinner coffee and cigarette ritual as a Trojan horse, slipping a very radical sensory innovation through the gate by wrapping it in a very familiar context. It appeals to those who "love experimenting with new foods and surprising culinary delights"; for some, the sheer novelty would be incentive enough to give it a go. But long-term success depends on people liking it enough to develop a whole new way of consuming food and experiencing taste. It's a great cultural challenge: "Until now, nobody had reliably put food in the mouth through breathing. First there were the hands, then chopsticks, then forks and spoons, and now [this]."

Moving from prototype to commercial product meant extensive engage-ment to find ways to address both technical and cultural challenges. To work out which variations might appeal most, they put on more experi-mentation evenings, serving up everything from cheese to mushrooms to exotic teas...

Edwards describes the audience engagement as "art-as-process" – one which involved a cultural shift as well as a scientific proof of concept. He went to arts hubs like the Cannes Film Festival, searching for contexts in which people would be sympathetic to cultural experimentation as well as to the celebration of the senses. "Our sales approach reflected a lab sensibility", says Edwards, in contrast to "a reasoned analysis of the market."

AeroDesigns now retails online and at The Lab Store in Paris – a concept design store that showcases products which "emerge from cultural experiments at frontiers of science". It also sells scoops of ice cream and frozen yoghurt wrapped in an edible skin, rather like a juicy grape, so that it doesn't melt in your hands and can be eaten without a spoon. This skin – a membrane comprising a mix of food particles bound with carbohydrates – is the key feature of what is today called WikiFood, another of Edwards' inventions, created in collaboration with the French designer Francois Azambourg. Ice-cream lovers can choose between coconut skin with a heart of mango, hazelnut with a heart of chocolate, or peanut with a heart of vanilla. Edwards notes that designers have always been inspired by forms found in nature; he takes inspiration from functionality. It may neither look nor taste like a grape skin but it works just like one.

A CONVERSATION WITH DAVID EDWARDS, FOUNDER AND DIRECTOR, QUANTUM DESIGNS

The work of biomedical engineer David Edwards spans science, culture and commerce. He teaches in the School of Engineering and Applied Sciences at Harvard University, and is a founding member of ArtScience Labs, a network of experimentation spaces across Europe, Africa and the US. He is also the founder and director of two innovation centers: Le Laboratoire, Paris and The Lab at Harvard University.

How does your work as a scientist relate to your work as an entrepreneur?

The companies of tomorrow don't exist today: they are in the process of being created. Our corporate and educational models are based on 19th century realities, and it is very hard to have anything other than a revenue-centric board. But I think the world of top-down has gone away. Today, value-creation is increasingly a local thing, and it's bottom-up. It has always been individuals that dream dreams and do things. Now, there are smaller groups that will come together and do things.

Whether we're talking about clothing or furniture or food, we're in a world where commercial value is anchored in the process of change: this process is as important as what the product looks like. For a long time, I was in the very traditional, academic world of university-based science, where "creators" are in a box, communicating with each other in their lab. Any innovation that would come out of their work was downstream. You would create, and then others would make and communicate. But there's a double difficulty with this model. First, there's a great frustration for the creator to not have any direct dialogue with the public, leading to failure in their attempts to create positive change. And for the public, it's frustrating, because they see the world is changing, and think, "Well, no one is really asking us". It leads to all sorts of personal or psychological impacts that are unforeseen and yet affect them. So, there's both an opportunity and a need for the public to be much more engaged in the creative process. Creators need this interaction: for us, it's a much more exciting world to be in, when you're bringing ideas forward and co-creating with members of the public. And they, too, want to be engaged in the creation of their future. I think this is the world we're moving towards. The most innovative products we have seen in recent years were very edited by the public. And for me, there's a relief in being part of this process – being part of a moment and having a stake in the future – as opposed to in a box.

How does innovation happen in the commercial world?

If you look at innovative ecosystems, they tend to have three coexisting value propositions. One is research and education: what Stanford brings to Silicon Valley. At the other end, there's a commercial value proposition: what Apple brings to Silicon Valley. And then there's a third proposition in between the two: an experimentation space, where people are paid to fail and take risks. That's the innovation "ecosystem" of Silicon Valley. In this ecosystem, it is hard to learn well without being allowed to fail, and hard to succeed commercially without passing through an experimental phase that brings lots of risk. This is the same sort of ecosystem found elsewhere, as with Broadway, which coexists with the experimental place Off-Broadway. Both the Valley and Broadway have a culture that validates experimentation – that is, risk and failure – and they innovate better because of this. It's that middle space that is so rare and important.

You teach a course called "How to create things and have them matter". What matters?

We spend a lot of time on this notion of what matters, from four points of view: cultural, commercial, humanitarian and research. From each viewpoint an idea may matter, if very differently. The goal is to figure out how your idea matters, and make it evolve fast enough so that it can survive and flourish. This process has some pain associated with it. If you are a writer of fiction, or an entrepreneur, you probably try to sell your dream: you try to convince an agent or editor, or an investor. The reaction to your pitch – rarely immediately favorable – gives you pause. You hopefully go back and rethink your idea and come back again. You've learned. Driven by your passion to get your idea out, you are learning how to make it matter. That's at the heart of being a creator: facing the fact that, a priori, most people likely don't think much of your idea. Until you make it somehow theirs as well. That takes a humble, empathetic person, which is ultimately what we try to create through teaching: better listeners, among other things!

Do aesthetics matter, and why?

I believe that the lab zone, this place within an innovative ecosystem where we do experiments and engage the public, is fundamentally a cultural place. We are not exactly delivering a service: we are exploring. And if the public comes into this place, whether it is Off-Broadway or a start-up in Silicon Valley, they are in a real way taking a risk with us. Aesthetics become a critical part of the language of interaction. Through how things are presented, even more than through how they "work" or "sound" or "perform", we express a kind of language, or culture, that fundamentally appeals to everyone in that experimental space, and rewards them in a sense for the risk they have taken to enter. This is how I think about aesthetics in the culture lab. The language of aesthetics binds us as creators to our audience, as co-creators.

We are very engaged in the exploration of new sensorial, often nutritional, experiences. I believe that there is a revolution afoot that parallels the information revolution, whereby we learned how to personalize information. This revolution is about personalizing nutrition to empower our very individual lives. But how can any of us know how everyone else wishes their nutritional experiences to be? We need to explore the question with the public, make some hypotheses, try out ideas; we need many come experiment with us, and we need to make this a lot of fun, and meaningful to everyone. We pay serious attention to the aesthetics of everything we design and do. And it works. Nutritional innovations are getting out there, curated with the public.

3 Ella's Kitchen

Food doesn't have to be innovative to stimulate our senses and expand our aesthetic horizons. Many of the most appetizing meals will be low-tech in preparation and locally sourced. This is the approach of Ella's Kitchen, a baby food brand which aims to help people explore their taste buds from their very first meals, so that they can develop a love of healthy, fresh produce that will last a lifetime. Its products are 100 per cent non-genetically modified and organic, certified where possible through the Soil Association, and it tries to keep air miles to a minimum (though struggles when it comes to mushy fruits like bananas and mangoes).

These ecological considerations aren't its unique selling point, though: it's the aesthetic experience of food for tots – through all five senses. "Because we know a love of good food is created by mealtimes that are tasty and fun, we have made the tiny taste bud journey fun to explore through different flavour [sic] combinations", the website explains. The "bright, shiny and sometimes squidgy packaging is designed to stimulate all the senses", and there is a range of resources besides to help parents expand their child's appreciation of the many different qualities of food – its colors, textures and even the sounds it makes as you shake it or chew it.

Like Harvard's David Edwards, the creators of Ella's Kitchen work very closely with their audience of parents and little ones, sounding them out on both what tastes good – to help them make "yummy new stuff" – and asking them what support the brand can offer to make mealtimes fun. This interaction is recognized in the many awards it has won, including the Loved By Parents Award for Best Baby Food and the Prima Baby Reader Platinum Award in 2011, and the Tesco Mum's Choice Gold Standard and Practical Pregnancy and Parenting Silver Award in 2012.

It helps that the brand was created by someone with experience of how un-fun feeding kids can be at times. In a video on the site, founder Paul Lindley speaks of the difficulties he experienced trying to wean his daughter, Ella, and her brother, Paddy. "I really understand how many parents will feel trying to get their kids to have good, healthy food", he says.

Alongside time spent talking to parents and little ones and trying to understand their needs, Ella's Kitchen did research with psychologists and supermarkets to understand the role of all five senses in developing healthy eating habits. When you're a food brand, taste may seem the most important sense of the five – but not necessarily, particularly if you're trying to get children to eat. The brand part-funded a study into the non-taste sensory properties of food by the School of Psychology and Clinical Language Sciences at the University of Reading. This study explored the "increasingly popular" assumption that familiarity with the sight, smell and feel of food will reduce resistance to it.[39] The researchers spent time with 55 children aged 12–36 months in their nursery environment – one which the infants associate with fun and games rather than meal-times. They offered them a series of sense-based activities involving fruit and vegetables, and assessed the impact of these activities on their willingness to taste the foods, compared to a control group. The activities explored the shape, size and color of the food when it was cut open; touching, squeezing, stroking, and smelling the food when it was cooked; singing a song about it; and hearing a story about it. The research team found that the children who took part in these activities in an informal play setting tasted significantly more of the vegetables they had been exposed to than a control group who were offered them in a mealtime context. They also found that the children identified the positive sensory experiences they'd enjoyed during the play session with that specific food, and not its wider food group: "While children who had taken part in activities involving figs were significantly more likely to taste this fruit, the intervention had no impact on children's willingness to consume fruit overall." They noted that further research is needed to identify which of the senses had the greatest impact, and whether the benefits of sensory exploration in a play setting are short-term – just until the next meal – or can be long lasting.

Ella's Kitchen offers a range of downloadable resources to help parents with the weaning challenge by appealing to all five of their child's senses. For example, the activity sheet "Sounds good" explains that a baby's hearing starts to develop before birth, and that babies and toddlers continue to develop their sense of hearing quickly in the months after birth. "As you'll have probably discovered, sounds can also be used to create excitement and anticipation when trying new foods", it prompts, suggesting parents create maracas and rattles by putting some pasta shapes or lentils in recycled plastic bottles, or showing the child how to snap carrot sticks to make a cracking sound. Another activity sheet suggests introducing "little noses to new smells" using scented sponges, made out of bits of bathroom sponge soaked in different smelling food liquids, such as vanilla essence, lemon juice or cranberry juice.

Ella's Kitchen recorded five songs about fruit and veg, each to the tune of a familiar nursery rhyme, in collaboration with the singer-songwriter and TV personality Rachel Stevens, and has created an educational program for nurseries, using play, games, songs, rhymes, and a practitioner's guide. The food products the brand sells – in their bright, colorful packaging – are also labelled by age range, to match the child's development. The mango and apple porridge for 4+ months is super smooth, whereas the strawberry, mango and banana porridge for 7+ months is textured, to encourage a little chewing. What Ella's Kitchen says loud and clear is that this isn't just about food that slips down easily enough: it's your child's first forage into their own sensory realm.

Vitality

In 1946, just after the Second World War, Pablo Picasso was staying with his lover Françoise Gilot in Antibes, a town on the French Mediterranean coast, built on the foundations of an Ancient Greek city. He got lucky: the curator of the Château Grimaldi – a family mansion-come-museum, containing some plaster casts and relics from the days of Napoleon – offered him the use of the top floor as a studio.[1] There, Picasso did a painting which he called *La Joie de Vivre*. The scene harks back to ideals of the good life as imagined by the Ancient Greeks – a pipe-playing fawn, a dancing nude, prancing goats – set against the staples of a 20th century sun-seeker's paradise: a sandy beach, blue sky, and a boat on the horizon. As Picasso's painting illustrates, how we feel and express an appetite for life varies across time and cultures, as well as from person to person.

The sense of physical and mental wellbeing that enhances our appetite for life and brings with it a heightened awareness of being alive is encapsulated in English by the word "vitality", from the Latin for "life". We are drawn towards experiences that help us nourish this appetite, through expressive activities like dance and song – as in Picasso's depiction – as well as sport, outdoor activities, and even quietening practices, such as yoga, prayer and meditation. Psychologists have defined vitality as a "positive feeling of aliveness and energy [which] refers to more than just being active, aroused or even having stored calorie reserves. [Rather] it concerns a specific psychological experience of possessing enthusiasm and spirit".[2]

For no one is vitality a given. You may have a clean bill of health as far as the doctor is concerned, and yet not feel energy and enthusiasm for life. You might be the epitome of vitality one day – you'll feel full of beans, get lots done, and then sit down with a friend who remarks on your joie de vivre; and yet on another day, you might feel rather drained, as though the wind's gone out of your sails… The degree to which people experience vitality is affected by many physical factors, such as sleep, diet, hormones and pain – but also by factors we associate with our emotional and spiritual lives: a sense of awe, being in love, having something to strive for, the gratification of achieving a goal.[3]

Not all these factors are beyond an individual's control – and they are certainly factors that a brand can influence. In yoga, practitioners regularly remind themselves of their desire to experience life to the full, setting this as their intention. What happens when a brand sets the same intention? How can it support its audience to feel this energy for life? This chapter explores what helps people to thrive in life, and asks how brands can make it easier for them.

Expressions of vitality

In Japan, a whole industry has sprung up since the 1980s around karaoke – and has become a major global export. While the emphasis on modesty in Japanese culture brings a reticence to perform on stage or take the microphone in bars, groups of friends and colleagues regularly sing their hearts out in soundproof rooms, with the aid of a few drinks ordered from their phone. Lucky Voice has brought this model to the UK, advocating singing as "a powerful tool to help us unlock feelings about our lives and let go" – a literal solution to the Brits' stiff upper lips. Alongside the booths and bars, it offers tailor-made solutions for businesses "looking to harness the pulling power of karaoke", and kits for people to sing at home, complete with a set of colorful microphones. On Twitter, Lucky Voice markets itself as the most "liberating, heart-racing, life-affirming karaoke experience on earth".

In many cultures, vitality is associated with color, and celebrations of life involve bright paints and costumes. In India, Hindis mark the arrival of spring, the season of birth, with the Holi festival in which people throw

In many cultures, vitality is associated with color

colored powders at each other and at holy temples – huge showers of red, blue, yellow, orange and pink. Many Native American, African, classical and pagan springtime celebration traditions have been incorporated into the pre-Lenten carnivals of Catholic countries across the world, most notably in the Caribbean and Latin America. In Brazil, this has led to an event of huge proportions: each year Rio de Janeiro's Carnival attracts around 5 million people, who come to watch parades of extravagant floats shimmy through the streets led by samba dancers and musicians with painted faces, headdresses, masks, feathers and flower garlands.

"Flower power" became the affirming life refrain of the Hippies in the 1960s. They took the lead from the American Beat poet Allen Ginsberg, who coined the term when he called on people to dress in vibrant colors and hand flowers to members of the public as a way of transforming anti-war protests into street theatre.[4] In the late 1970s, love, life and color became associated with the Gay Rights movement[5] – expressed through carnivalesque Pride marches and symbols such as the Rainbow Flag. The original eight-stripe flag was designed by the activist and artist Gilbert Baker, who assigned a meaning to each of the colors, beginning with hot pink for sexuality and red for life. (Hot pink was later discarded as the fabric proved too expensive to source.)

The psychedelic drug culture of the Hippie movement was partly driven by the desire to experience life at its extremes, stimulating the mind to reach states often compared to religious ecstasy or meditative trance. Other thrill-seekers jump out of planes or climb sky scrapers. While in 1974, the high-wire artist Philippe Petit walked and even danced, for a good 40 minutes, between the Twin Towers of New York's World Trade Center. In a TED talk, Petit describes his early love of magic and his desire to "cheat the impossible", which he achieves through a combination of his own passion, perfectionism and faith – and the amazing "human symphony" of others clapping in encouragement. "By inspiring ourselves, we inspire others", he says.[6]

C H A L L E N G E   Y O U R   B R A N D

- How can your brand inspire people to reach new heights in their experience of life?
- If your brand were to paint a picture of vitality, what colors and images would it use?
- How does your brand invite people to cheer each other on?

What brands can learn from samba

These examples – even the man alone on the wire – illustrate how individual vitality is enhanced by the exuberance of those around us. It has an infectious quality. If brands can play a role in supporting people to experience vitality, it will be both through very personalized interaction with individuals and through bringing people together in the sort of cultural movements described above. Professor Henry Jenkins, an expert in participatory culture at the University of Southern California, argues that American culture has a lot to learn from the "varied and multiple ways" in which the samba schools of Rio de Janeiro "enable meaningful participation for all of their community members". He describes his perception of their impact on their lives beyond the dance floor:

> The Samba Schools are embedded within particular communities – most often in the Favelas, which is where the poorest of the poor live in Rio. Upon entering these communities, as an outsider, one is impressed both by the density of the population and by the vibrancy of community life. Everywhere you look, people are gathered together, engaged in conversations, and around the edges, you can see a range of expressive activities. For me, the creativity fostered by the Samba Schools is also visible in the graffiti and street art which adorns walls all over the city. And the playfulness can be seen in the boys and girls who are trying to conduct kite battles just outside the city center.[7]

So how do the Samba Schools do it, and what can brands learn? In the chapter on community, I spoke of the importance of a shared space which can be interpreted as the people using it wish. Jenkins notices the difference that the Samba School space makes straight away, describing it as "incredibly open and designed to insure sociability", but also flexible, allowing people to move easily between observing and participating. He remarks that, "There is no decisive moment when participants step from watching to dancing. The music pulls at you – you start to sway your hips or nod along without even fully realizing it." The karaoke clubs of Japan and even organized marches do a similar job: they create a space in which it's ok to sing, dance or shout, to express yourself beyond everyday social norms.

Jenkins then moves onto a more "provocative" aspect of the experience: what he calls the "participation police". These mock-officers in uniform go round the floor rounding up anyone who's not participating in the fun and giving them a little talking-to about the traditions of the community. Jenkins instinctively objects to this implication of forced participation, although – given the officers' willingness to accept his "peripheral participation", which he demonstrates by wearing a t-shirt and a grin – he is able to laugh it off. He takes the opportunity to make a point about the importance of removing barriers to participation (speaking of education in particular), asserting that we should "build in active mechanisms which repeatedly encourage and solicit" the involvement of people on the peripheries.

So here is another role for brands: beyond supporting the creation of spaces in which people can experience and express their love of life, and supporting cultural movements within them, they can also offer support to individuals to overcome their inhibitions. To achieve this, brands need to look beyond their immediate space to the wider context, asking what might stop people from joining in. Barriers might be infrastructural, such as transport or finance, or they may be a question of social exclusion and prejudice. Any brand looking to enhance vitality without first encouraging openness internally will have a steep hill to climb. While it is important for any brand to build up a clear picture of the audience it would like to reach, if it defines this too narrowly it runs the risk of alienating others, exposing itself to both criticism and resentment. A brand can win respect and recognition for supporting people from diverse backgrounds to become part of its community, and its following will be more likely to act as advocates on its behalf, nudging their friends onto the dance floor.

CHALLENGE YOUR BRAND

- Who is standing at the edge of your brand's dance floor?
- What might prevent people from joining in?
- How could your brand help to break down the barriers to participation?

The buzz and beyond

"Vitality" has become something of a buzzword for civic bodies when assessing the value of cultural and artistic activities in urban areas. This is a good thing, as long as they also bear in mind that other socioeconomic factors, and notably public health, must complement the arts in order to make a difference to the vitality of individuals at scale. If not, the risk is that vitality is experienced as a distant hum over the heads of many, and in the hearts of just a few.

A collaboration of government bodies, brands, academics and cultural institutions, led by the Goldhirsh Foundation under the banner LA2050, collates data on cultural and artistic activities in Los Angeles: what opportunities there are, as well as levels of participation. It aims to assess the "vibrancy and strength of the region", asserting both the direct economic impacts and the reputational benefits for LA as an "iconic" place. The status quo, a 2013 report found, is healthy: Los Angeles has more art establishments per capita than any other metropolitan area in the US, and the highest concentration of working artists and art professionals. However, it also expresses concern that the region lacks any coherent policy for nurturing the arts, and that high living costs are discouraging the next generation of artists from moving in.[8] The CEO of the Los Angeles County Museum of Art has said that LA could "be passed by in terms of long-term recognition and vitality if it doesn't consolidate its artistic production quality with lasting infrastructure".

In 2012, the Mayor of London launched the World Cities Culture Report, which includes a section dedicated to the "cultural vitality and diversity" of 12 major cities, focusing on their street life: the night clubs, dance halls, bars, restaurants, and the communities they represent. (There are separate sections for the institutionalized arts sectors, including performing arts, literary culture and film.) "These factors might be thought of as measuring the 'buzz' of a city", the authors write. "Buzz matters because it shapes many of the perceptions of a city for residents and tourists alike, and it may also have beneficial economic effects." The report compares the number of carnivals, festivals, bars, clubs, restaurants and dance halls across the 12 cities – admitting that defining these venues precisely is a challenge. Shanghai and São Paolo were judged to have a particularly lively night life, while Tokyo has by far the highest number of eating places, at 150,000, including the most Michelin-starred restaurants. The report also explores the diversity of each city's population, in terms of foreign-born population and international students and tourists – asserting that innovation stems from "the meeting of cultural forms".[9]

The rising recognition of the economic benefits of "buzz" presents an opportunity for brands to demonstrate their social and cultural value. But while a brand that opens a chain of cocktail bars in a thriving spot might get a nod from London's Mayor Boris Johnson, it will need to do more than this to have any lasting impact on the vitality of people living there. The question brands need to ask is how they can bring the highs of a night out into people's daily lives, without simply giving them a hangover. How can they build on the potential for human capital created by all these vibrant venues? To do this, they will need to dig deeper into their audience's experience, getting right down into the intricacies of different communities, their habits and their desires. How long does it take for the colors of the carnival to fade? Aside from pink powdered paint, what else might help people to see *la vie en rose*?

The strange case of Dr Health and Mr Vitality

Few scenes offer a more striking contrast to a carnival than the white walls and sterility of a hospital. And yet health is one of the most important factors in vitality, and enhancing quality of life is one of the primary goals of medicine. However, health practitioners, brands and services can sometimes lose sight of this, focusing on the treatment of a specific concern. This is most evident in the work of pharmaceuticals, which market drugs with licenses for limited applications, and sometimes fail to publicize possible side effects sufficiently for the user to make a sound judgement about whether they will end up better or worse off. In public services, treatment with a view to cure and longevity can take precedence over care and wellbeing, a concern that has been raised within the UK's National Health Service. A combination of pressure on time and resources, over-stretched nurses and rigid quantifiable targets can push the emotional and mental impacts of hospitalization out of the picture when it comes to delivery. In addition, a training system that prompts doctors to specialize in specific parts or functions of the body can detract from their understanding of the system as a whole, and in particular the correlation between physical and mental health. The mind is allocated its own specialist field, psychiatry.

Back in 1961, Dr Rene Dubos of the Rockefeller Institute for Medical Research delivered a series of lectures at Yale University entitled "Medical

Futures and Human Populations". He proposed that "the time is right for a new departure that would focus research on the mechanisms linking body and mind. Everyone knows that what happens in the mind affects profoundly the functions of the body." He warned of the importance of developing "adaptive protective mechanisms" to ensure long-term health – instead of focusing on the treatment of problems as they arise. He described Western medicine as a system that prompts mankind to "run from cover to cover like a tracked animal" – however fast we run, this is hardly a portrait of vitality. Remaining alive is one thing; experiencing life to the full is another.[10]

Brands can help to bridge the gap between health and vitality. They can offer individuals support to see how various aspects of their lifestyle affect their wellbeing. They can bring together resources to help people make the best choices. And they can help to create cultures and communities that make healthy living desirable. A series of recommendations to improve mental health and wellbeing across the population, created by UK think-tank the new economics foundation (nef), offers a starting point. nef's "Five ways to wellbeing" are aimed at individual members of the public, prompting them to: connect with others; be active; enjoy time outdoors; learn a new skill; and give.[11] Dax Lovegrove, Head of Business and Industry at WWF-UK, believes brands could work with individuals in all five areas. For an example, he points to parkrun, which ticks four of the boxes ("give" is an optional extra). It's a syndicate of free running clubs open to everyone, funded through partnership and advertising. It encourages people to participate in a weekly five-kilometre run in their local park, and offers resources to help them get started, from water to warm-up exercises. Parkrun started in the UK, and is now operating in Australia, Denmark, Poland, South Africa and the US. Its sponsorship scheme has attracted major sports brands, such as adidas, offering them a direct way to engage with the people they want to reach. "It's a very authentic experience, with a massive social network", says Lovegrove. "Families come along with their kids, dogs can even be dumped off with volunteers, and then they all have a coffee afterwards."

The strength of parkrun is that it combines a way to improve your physical health with access to community culture. This is something that many brands offering health and wellbeing-related products and services – from pharmaceuticals to whole foods to fitness classes – fail to do. Some may lack the resources. Others simply haven't recognized the benefits, taking time to consider what vitality means for their brand.

Unilever is one brand that identifies vitality as a goal, aiming "to meet everyday needs for nutrition, home hygiene and personal care with brands that help people feel good, look good and get more out of life". The blurb on the website explains how particular brands do this: "Flora helps keep hearts healthy, a cup of PG Tips refreshes you, Magnum gives you an indulging treat … Sure gives you unbeatable protection, and hair washed and styled with Sunsilk looks great but also gives you confidence to take on life."[12] However, while each brand arguably contributes something towards helping a person feel or look good (and these are not the same), they limit their proposition to one aspect of a person's wellbeing. Low-cholesterol margarine may be good for the heart, but chocolate and ice cream arguably have other impacts on it. As a house of brands, Unilever has the opportunity to develop a more coherent strategy: the challenge will be to encourage each individual brand to see its own offer in relation to a person's life as a whole.[13]

The private health insurance and services provider PruHealth offers its clients a more holistic approach through its Vitality program, which recognizes the relationship between lifestyle and health. Through Vitality, PruHealth offers its members a wide range of lifestyle benefits by bringing together commercial and non-profit partners, and rewards them for using the products and services on offer through a points-based scheme. PruHealth implies that the positive impacts of these supposedly healthy choices on the individual's wellbeing deserve to be recognized through financial savings – a lower premium for their health insurance cover, or a discount on healthcare services. PruHealth offers a personalized approach: every member completes an online Health Review to help assess their current state of health, and the brand uses this to create a personal plan, which brings together diet, fitness, health problems (such as smoking), relaxation and entertainment. PruHealth's partners respond to the various points on the plan. Individuals can increase their vitality status, from bronze through to platinum, by earning points – for example, for diet by buying products from Sainsbury's healthy foods range; for "wellbeing" by visiting a Champney's Spa; or for "getting active" by joining an LA Fitness gym (where they can sign up for a Fitbug to track their progress), buying a bike from Evans Cycles, or spending a day out at one of the National

Trust properties. It would be interesting to know to what extent the users of PruHealth Vitality actually experience greater energy for life. Do the points they earn make more of a difference to their premium than to their positivity?

To find out, PruHealth would need to encourage its members to reflect on their experience and share their observations – and perhaps also their Fitbug data – openly. Meaningful answers would depend on the trust its members place in its intentions as a brand. Can they really trust the brand to respond with an appropriate level of care and support, if they take the trouble to answer such intimate questions as "How well do you really feel, not just in your body but in your heart and soul?"

A pair of London-trained osteopaths, Ed and Lucy Paget, set up their company Intrinsi, which is based in Calgary, Canada, to encourage exactly this sort of exchange. They don't just treat the ailing; they also welcome people to come and see them when they're feeling fine. Why would you do that? Because "your body is complex, your goals and experience are unique – you want a team of health professionals that take all of this into account and will work together to address every aspect of your wellbeing".[14] Osteopathy is an alternative school of medicine that teaches an integrated approach to mind, body and spirit, exploring how the structure and anatomy of the body relates to its functionality and to an individual's wellbeing. However, many osteopaths take the skeleton as a starting point and stick pretty close to it, with the result that they are mainly approached to treat back pain. The Pagets didn't want to be pigeonholed in this way. They set up Intrinsi "to deliver health and to educate people about just how amazing their bodies are". Their brand strapline is "Don't just live, thrive".

A CONVERSATION WITH ED PAGET, CO-FOUNDER, INTRINSI[15]

What do you think people actually want for their health?

We did a survey and got about 500 people in our database to tell us what they want from us. Advice on exercise and nutrition were top of the list – admittedly they were choosing from a range of options that we had provided, including more hands-on treatment, preventative measures and so on. But this made us question everything we had learned in our training with regards to patient management. The school of osteopathy where we had trained in London had taken the view: "Don't give them exercises because they won't do them. Don't give them dietary advice because they won't follow it..." Osteopathy is quite traditional and this sort of dogma gets passed down from the lecturers to the students, and the students then become lecturers and pass it down. But by questioning it, we feel we are more able to give people what they want. Some healthcare professionals say things like, "Patients want a private room", or, "They want to see the same person every time", and those things might well be true, but we like to test it to find out whether it is true for each patient. So we ask them, through surveys, interviews and feedback.

Do you use social media?

We have a YouTube channel with a lot of hits and a lot of followers – for an osteopathy practice, that is! We have one video on scoliosis that has people from all over the world interacting with us. It's amazing to be helping people in other countries without actually meeting them. We have Twitter and Facebook, and I'm on LinkedIn. I do think it brings in more patients, but it's really about sharing the information. What we want to do through these channels is create a following. We have a "tribe" concept: a group of followers to whom we can say, "We want a bit of help to create a retreat space", and of the 5000 people on our lists, a few come forward to help us. Not so long ago I did a course in the US, at the Gray Institute, and I asked one guy there why he was on the course, and he said, "I'll do anything the Gray Institute does, because I just think it's awesome." And I thought, that's where I want Intrinsi to be. I want real buy-in.

Will this tribal movement have any positive impact on your customers' health?

If you look around the world, there are "blue zones" where people live to an age that's higher than the global average. There's Sardinia, Okinawain in Japan, Loma Linda in California.

It's my understanding that these zones don't have much in common: the nutrition is different, the way in which people exercise is different. The one thing they do seem to share is that the older the person gets, the more involved in the community they are, and the more respected within the community they are. I wonder whether or not in this Western world of minimal community we can offer through our brand something that's bigger than the person, that provides a community. There is research that shows people live longer if they believe in something bigger than them...

Why would people want to engage with a brand in that way?

I think it works because our interests are aligned with theirs, but we can take the time to go off and research the things they want to know about, and provide a channel for them to experience it. We meet so many people who are interested in nutrition and exercise, but they also have a downtown job nine to five, and so they don't have time to look into it themselves. We synthesize the information and then deliver it in a shorter time, through workshops.

How are you building your following?

We have some strategic partners in the community with which we do promotions and cross-referrals: there are yoga studios, personal trainers, a company called The Fitness Table, a company selling mattresses tailored to your physiology, and so on. If we like what they do, we write a review of their service in our newsletter and stamp their photo with our logo and "Intrinsi approved" – so that people can see that we're going out into the community, finding other services and testing them. We're doing the research for them. The idea is that people can come via the Intrinsi brand and find an approved massage therapist, or personal trainer and so on.

Is there any financial benefit for people who follow your advice?

We looked into that, but it's hard when you're dealing with small businesses.

What does "Intrinsi approved" mean to people?

It's like a friend who you'd ask about movies, and if they say "You have to go and see this movie", you go. They're not a film critic, they just give good advice. You might have another friend who you know doesn't give good advice, and if they see a movie, you don't... So we want to be the friend who gives good advice for health and wellness. If people trust us, they might like what we like.

What does vitality mean to you?

Vitality is something we talk about in osteopathy quite a lot. If you put your hands on a person's head or body, and if it doesn't feel "alive" then it has decreased vitality. If a person had a neck injury and their neck is stiff and tight, their blood flow can be affected, so we talk about restoring vitality before we restore function. So, you would free up some of these blocks to get the blood, the "vitality" flowing.

So, if I put my hands on someone's head, all I feel is hair and scalp. How do you feel vitality?

It's quite hard for even osteopaths to get this! It's hard to imagine – but if you put your hand on a lump of meat, it's not only cold but there's no life expression. If you warm up the meat and put your hand on it, you would still know that it is not alive. When you touch someone's head, you're not really feeling their pulse, or their breath: you're feeling their life-force. So in osteopathy, we talk about a cranial rhythm: the pumping of the spinal fluid around the brain and up and down the spine. It's a slight expansion and contraction within every cell. This primary respiratory mechanism is found within every living cell – in plants, trees, even in protoplasmic structures, like slime. They all have this expansion and contraction, which occurs every 10–15 seconds across most living organisms. So an osteopath is feeling for this rhythm, and it changes according to a person's health in quite subtle ways. If a person is depressed, you may still feel the rhythm, but it won't be as strong. In my experience, when I feel the skulls of people who are depressed, they have a sluggish rhythm.

Are people aware of their rhythms?

I've noticed that people who ride horses usually are! I think it's because they know that if their mind and body aren't doing the same thing, the horse will reflect it. And so, somehow they're more in tune with their mind and body. I've had horse riders come to me and say, "I'm not happy with how the horse is turning. I know it's not the horse, it must be me." So we treat the horse rider, and the horse's behavior changes. The rider understands that the horse is a reflection of their own vitality.

How important is profit to your business?

In most healthcare professions, profit is an ugly word, but profit allows us to take the business where we want it to go. A patient of ours who works with non-profit organizations and helps them to get clear on their mission, offered to help us. So we told her everything about our vision, employee satisfaction, client satisfaction; we put it all up on this eight-foot blackboard in our house and showed her, and she said, "I'm going to circle one word on this board, which do you think it's going to be?" And we said, wellness or health. And she walked over and circled profit, because – she said – you can't do any of this unless you make money. That was five years ago. So we got a business coach from the US, who told us that in most companies payroll is 30–35 per cent, then roughly 30 per cent management, and 30 per cent profit. At the time, we were taking just 5 per cent as profit. We decided to try and change our model. We broke away from industry standards and aim to pay our employees a salary, instead of giving them a percentage cut. So, if they see two people or twenty in a day, they'll get paid the same. That way, we can ask them to contribute to the brand through social media, or do in-house lectures, or do a customer survey; they are then invested in the brand, because their job depends on the brand, and not just on their own clientele. This is something that doesn't happen very much in osteopathy: almost everyone is paid on commission. But many business advisors think that a salary model is the future of osteopathy, so I think we're on the cutting edge of that.

Why does it matter that your osteopaths are engaged with the brand?

We want them be role models for health. The last thing you want to see is an osteopath with a bad back, or a nutritionist that's overweight! It's good to be a role model. So we do a weekly education seminar where we take turns to present to the team our area of interest; we also bring in external speakers to talk about their views on health and brand management, and relate this to how we can help patients. We offer health benefits to our staff: they can see anyone in the clinic, including our naturopathic doctor, for one session a month for free, so that they can deal with any problems. If we work through a long and healthy life, if we're still working in our 70s and 80s, I think that could be quite inspirational. There's an American holistic therapist called Paul Chek whose line is, "If you go to the doctor, ask them to take their shirt off (if it's a guy, that is) and if you're not impressed by what you see, then leave!"

CHALLENGE YOUR BRAND

- Does your brand address just one part of the body, or does it treat each person as a whole?
- How does culture affect the mental and physical health of your audience?
- How could your brand reward vitality?

Pictures of health

Brands can both endorse or question social norms and play a role in establishing new ones. Adam Lowry, co-founder and CEO of Method, believes that this is a power every brand has, merely by virtue of its public presence and its purpose as a communications medium. He explains:

> You could make the argument that every single brand sells a philosophy. Now, some of them are very uninteresting and not particularly aligned

with social good, or aspirational, but they're still a philosophy. More and more every day, living in a world of information, we're surrounded by brands, and brands have messages that they carry. Products are just a manifestation of their philosophy.

Vitality is an attitude, the result of mental empowerment as well as physical wellbeing, and so the message a brand carries will affect the vitality of the people it touches perhaps to a greater degree than the products it offers. A brand's message may prove the key to helping people connect with a community, set out on adventures, or enhance their aesthetic life. Its philosophy – the way in which it talks about a better life and the visions it creates – could shape the aspirations of its audience. Some visions may be detrimental to their journey towards vitality: negative body images, status-led notions of success, gender-stereotyping in portrayals of a happy home. A brand with a careless approach to the philosophy underlying its products and services may find that it is at odds with its declared intention. For instance, the dietary benefits of a beautifully produced collection of recipes for healthy, energizing food could be offset by the psychological negatives caused by related images of an overtly sexualized woman preparing them. Or a subscription to a sequence of body-shaping gym classes could well tone your tummy or bulk out your biceps, but leave you permanently dissatisfied when you glance at the tanned and muscular demi-gods on the adverts.

The approach Dove has taken to redefining norms of beauty is a step in the right direction (see Chapter Two for a wider discussion of this), but its success is ultimately undermined by the less questioning philosophies of other brands in Unilever's portfolio. For example, whereas Dove asks women to recognize and appreciate their natural beauty, Sunsilk prompts them to feel dissatisfied with their "look" and so to change their hair color or straighten their curls: "Imagine how bored you would be if you wore only one shade of clothes every day? Or if you styled yourself only in one way? That's because style is all about experimenting with different looks."[16] Dove's ability to make a difference to how women perceive their own beauty will depend on its ability to influence not only other brands within Unilever, but also the non-Unilever products sitting beside its own on the supermarket shelf. Indeed, for Dove to succeed in the cultural shift it aspires to, it will need to engineer a whole social movement, bringing its competitors along with it, and engaging other brand sectors that shape how women think and feel about themselves. Fashion, hospitality and tourism might be obvious ones to target, but Dove could also work with education providers looking to shape the aspirations of young girls, or with arts institutions. Together, they will need to engage marketing vehicles, such as magazines and digital media.

In China, Dove is already moving in this direction. It ran a workshop on healthy relationships in collaboration with China Dream, which, as I describe more fully in the Introduction, aims to shape the aspirations of China's emergent middle class by establishing a new set of social norms. One of its target areas is health and wellness: it aims to instill values such as "balance" – between body and mind, urban life and nature, work and play – and "vibrant living" at all stages of life, through mental sharpness and physical fitness. I asked Founder and Chairperson Peggy Liu for further examples of how China Dream is being realized through collaboration, and she described two programs. "A New Way to Eat" is an ambitious initiative to redesign nutritional guidelines to show people how to eat in a way that's good for you and good for the planet.

> We're working on the research now with an influential consortium of experts and academia. Our goal is to get this into school curriculum, create delicious recipes for school meals within budget, and influence ready meal companies to experiment with new product ranges based on these principles. One of the key challenges is that nutritional experts don't talk with sustainable agriculture experts, so much of the initial work is to bridge the dialogue.

China Dream is also working with the global hospitality, foodservice and healthcare service and product provider Ecolab to design and distribute a brochure offering "10 Tips for Safe & Healthy Restaurants".[17]

CHALLENGE YOUR BRAND

- What is the philosophy behind your brand? Is it in line with your products and services?
- Which social norms does your brand reinforce? Which does it question?
- How could your brand work with culture and media to shape how people feel and think?

The infrastructure of vitality

Our perspectives are shaped by culture, but they are also framed by context. Liu is well aware that health and wellbeing depend on environmental and infrastructural factors – such as access to water, green space and clean air – as much as on cultural perceptions and contexts. "Think about the recent pollution issues we've been having in China: Beijing had an episode in January [2013] where it was 700+ on the Air Pollution Index[18]: that's off the scale of the World Health Organization", she remarks. Brands with a commitment to health and vitality need to look beyond a person's body and mind to the health of their surroundings. They may have a role to play in contributing to it, through roof gardens and urban farming plots, for example. The impact of our surroundings on our physical and mental wellbeing is something Intrinsi's founders have taken into account. The wall paint in their studios is free from volatile organic compounds; clay helps to regulate the humidity; plants purify the air.

Brands also have a role in shaping shared spaces and unlocking access to resources that can promote vitality. Intrinsi has created a community garden which clients can enjoy and where the practitioners grow their own food. Parkrun and its sponsors demonstrate the value a resource as simple as a public park can offer a brand.

Catarina Tagmark, Vice President Corporate Brand and Design at Siemens AG, extends this logic right across the city, and every aspect of common infrastructure. She recognizes that a brand lives and breathes in the same world as its audience: it is not a puppeteer looking down on their world as upon a toy stage. Rather, it is a group of people living within that world, and working towards a particular goal. She explained to me why this infrastructure is just as important to a brand working in a space as it is to the community living there:

> Siemens is involved in projects of huge scale that last a long time, such as solving commuter problems through improvements to trains or walkways. It's not a question of "come in, set up, leave". If we are bidding to build a bridge, we will also walk on it; we will share the outcome. This is why a mayor or a commissioner will trust us, and why Siemens has been around for so long in many markets. Both as a professional working for that company and as a citizen living in the area, it's in my interest to

be engaged in my surroundings as a citizen: I will walk through that park or past that hospital every day.

Tagmark emphasizes the importance of the human side of a brand. It's not just the name on the billboard, it's the sum of its people. Their wellbeing and vitality is crucial to the brand's potential to enhance the lives of others. They may not be the ones at the front of the stage with the microphone, but that doesn't matter. If her brand was a rock band, Tagmark says, she would "do the vocals and play the funny little instruments that nobody else has heard of, but which make all the difference to the end result. And she would enjoy it immensely."

Desire-led brands in action

Brands can thrive on the contagious nature of vitality, both through the energy of the people who work for it or more directly: offering people a context to sing or dance themselves, as we saw earlier in the chapter with Lucky Voice and the Samba Schools. They can encourage people to take up activities that help them to feel good about themselves, like Parkrun, or they can support people to access such opportunities, by focusing on the surrounding infrastructure, like Siemens, or challenging discrimination.

Brands can help people to realize the connections between their mental, physical and emotional health, and to see how their own health is affected by their environment. They can create shared resources, such as gardens and green roofs, boosting vitality for everyone.

Perhaps the most important role a brand can play is to rebrand life as something to love every day. They can ask people when they last felt real joy in simply *being*, awakening their desire for vitality, and then helping them to find it in themselves.

These three case studies explore how brands are making vitality their mission by engaging with people, finding ways to understand what "feeling good" in body and mind means to them, and then co-creating responses. Here are some key questions to consider as you read about them:

- How does this brand ask what "vitality" means to its audience?
- How is it working with people to increase their sense of vitality?

• How does it engage with people in a holistic way, as mind, body and spirit?

Case studies

1   Zumba Fitness

> Oh, yes, I was freaked. I was hooked. An hour of Zumba was like an instant anti-depressant. It was better than my favorite once-a-year cocktail, the Perce-tini: half a Percocet and a martini. And it turned out I was—*throw your hands in the ay-ah!*—a good dancer. Girlfriends, ladies, mamis: I had Moves.

Alex Kuczynski also has Words, admittedly. A *New York Times* reporter and the author of a bestseller, she could write enthusiasm to order. But this isn't advertorial: it's her own testimony in *Harper's Bazaar*.[19] The testimonies of other fans may not be quite so exquisitely crafted, but communicate a similar level of enthusiasm: "No sentence can ever completely explain how you feel" … "I had so much fun, there was energy, there was passion" … "I feel awesome all the time, I feel energized, I want to work out, it's no longer a chore".[20]

How has Zumba created such an irresistible formula for vitality? By responding to the enthusiasm of its audience from the very start. What is now a global movement began in a community gym in Columbia, where Alberto "Beto" Perez was teaching an aerobics class. One day, the story goes, he turned up without the standard tunes, so he dug in his bag, pulled out some salsa and merengue, and did what he could.[21] The improvised class became such a success that he tried to export it, eventually persuading a fitness instructor in Miami to let him give her a one-on-one lesson. Passers-by stopped to see what was going on and – as he tells it – simply couldn't help joining in, and so he got the green light. The class quickly became the most popular in the health club.[22] One woman there was so enthusiastic about "Beto's talent" that she told her son – Alberto Perlman, an analyst at a McKinsey spin-off – to approach him. He did, and the two men hit it off on the spot. Perlman brought in another friend, Alberto Aghion, who was running an internet company and keen to find a new opening after the burst of the dot.com bubble. Between them, the three

Albertos had business nous, web development skills, and enough vitality to get the whole world on the dance floor. Or they believed they did, because, as Perlman tells it, none of them had any money to invest. And critically, others (including Perlman's mother) believed it too.[23]

Its rapid growth as a brand is partly down to its business model, which is very open to franchise. "Bring Zumba to your facility", the website encourages gyms, dance halls and other community venues across the world. To get started all they need to do is find a qualified instructor, and the website lists all those qualified to teach, with their location. The website prompts Zumba enthusiasts to train as instructors, becoming part of the brand and helping to develop it within their own community.

The brand declares its mission to be "changing lives", and as part of that it values the career opportunities it can offer. "The same thrilling energy we deploy worldwide comes to life inside our offices", its marketers claim. "Our work environment is challenging, engaging and incredibly social, and we value – and reward! – passion, accountability and creative thinking."

And what does the brand offer? It's basically a fitness class, but with the emphasis more on fun than on fitness and on the music rather than your muscles. The music includes Samba (little surprise) – but also many other dances of Latin and Caribbean origin: Merengue, Salsa, Reggaeton, Rhumba, Flamenco, Calypso and more. Like the Samba Schools of Brazil, Zumba offers an inclusive, community-based party. And, like a carnival, it's intended to feel like a celebration of life.

The brand has also sought to understand the desires of people at all ages, appealing to a much wider audience than the outgoing types with tanned and toned bodies that might typically be associated with a Latin-themed dance club. It has designed classes that take into account varying levels of fitness, coordination and confidence.

Zumba Fitness acknowledges that not everyone is looking to tone up: many come for the social side or the sheer feel-good factor. There's Zumbini, which is designed to offer a bonding experience for parents and their up to three-year-olds, in which they "wiggle, sing and learn together". If you're a teenager looking to build your self-confidence and still hoping to find your coordination, there's Zumbatomic. And then there's Zumba Gold, which offers "modified, low impact moves for older adults" who want to stay active without putting too much pressure on tired joints or straining their hearts.

The company is smart to recognize the commercial potential of "retiring baby boomers [who] account for 28 percent of the [US] population and 40 percent of total consumer demand – spending $2 trillion in goods and services each year." It also estimates that, by 2040, one in four Americans will be over the age of 65. For this generation, parents and children, the offer of a community experience in a feel-good setting may well be more important than a toned tummy and the calorie count.

Zumba Fitness claims its classes reach 14 million people in 151 countries. Its brand has reached further still: a YouTube video of a class uploaded in 2006 has been seen by more than 38 million; another, uploaded in 2011, showing people doing Zumba in iconic places like Sydney Harbour, has been seen by over 7 million. Zumba Fitness has also produced a series of video games for Xbox and Wii, where players can learn different dance styles and new routines at home, led by Zumba creator Beto.

Zumba is a beautifully simple concept, built on clear evidence that the combination of music and movement in a vibrant social space helps people to feel good in body, mind and spirit. But crucial to its success is its adaptability to the specific desires of various age groups and local communities. It co-creates each class with its audience, and supports them to recreate it in their communities, homes and offices.

2 Special Olympics

The vitality of one person can be influenced by the expectations of others. The "symphony" of applause from the crowd below helped Philippe Petit to keep walking the wire strung between the Twin Towers, when his own self-belief might otherwise have let him down. If someone you respect believes you are capable of embracing life with every fibre in your body, you are likely to rise to the challenge, and perhaps even surpass their expectations. But just as encouragement can make all the difference to success, the lack of it can prove a barrier. If the expectations of those around you are low, your ability to live life to the full will be diminished.

This was observed by Eunice Kennedy Shriver, who saw that if people with intellectual disabilities (also referred to as learning disabilities) were offered the same opportunities as everyone else – demonstrating belief in their potential – they could accomplish far more than others thought possible. She set up a summer camp in her backyard to show others she was right, inviting children to participate in a variety of sports. This was 1962. In 1968, the first International Special Olympics were held in Chicago. At the Opening Ceremony, Shriver remarked that the event proves that children with intellectual disabilities can be exceptional athletes, realizing their potential through sport.

Today, the Special Olympics offers 32 sports. Its profile is such that US President Barack Obama and First Lady Michelle committed to serving as Honorary Chairs of the 2015 Special Olympics World Games, which will be hosted in Los Angeles. Mayor Eric Garcetti recognized the honor with the following statement: "When 7000 Special Olympics athletes from 170 countries march into the Coliseum in two years, the spotlight will not only be on Los Angeles – a city that stands for diversity and inclusion – but will shine brightly on the mission of Special Olympics in highlighting the talents of those with intellectual disabilities". Garcetti also recognized the "major" contribution the Special Olympics will make to the city's economy, "generating more than $400 million in economic impact". He expects the 2015 Games to be the largest sports-and-humanitarian event anywhere in the world that year, and the biggest single event in Los Angeles since the 1984 Olympic Games, with half a million spectators.

The Special Olympics invites people to raise their expectations of themselves and pursue their dreams. But to make this possible, it must influence the attitudes of those around them, those who could either offer support or stand in their way: it must change mindsets across the world by establishing a new culture which promotes acceptance and focuses on ability. The brand measures its success in this through stories rather than through numbers:

> We know it works when we hear that a young Special Olympics athlete raised in an institution in India is visited and congratulated by government officials after earning a gold medal at World Games. When a US city posts a highway sign boasting that the town is the home of a Special Olympics runner. And when a new world of acceptance is opened

to a Cote d'Ivoire athlete following a successful competition: "I have become the star of my neighborhood and our church, I, the one who used to be rejected...!"

The Special Olympics aims to remove obstacles to vitality for some of the most vulnerable people in the world. Intellectual disabilities are often accompanied by financial difficulties, physical disabilities, mental health problems, social exclusion, restricted educational opportunities, and limited access to pleasures many take for granted – such as travel, entertainment and the arts. For people in such circumstances to radiate vitality may seem impossible, but it's not.

In a blog on the Special Olympics website, Winston Maxino recounts how he "chanced upon a charming athlete ... beaming with joy", whose happiness inspired him to take photos of her. He later met her again and remembers her warm handshake and excitement. She was Stephanie Wiegel, a snowboarder with Down syndrome, who won a medal in the 2013 Special Olympics World Winter Games in PyeongChang, Republic of Korea. The vitality of such a person will influence the perceptions of anyone they meet – but their exclusion from many mainstream social networks means many people never have the opportunity. To reach the mainstream, the Special Olympics needs a strong brand, and the current Chairman and CEO Tim Shriver, the son of Eunice, is in no doubt of this: "The evolution and progress of our Movement have benefited by the alignment of our brand around the world. We have common language, an enhanced visual identity, a strong brand architecture and a deeply profound experience that is truly transformative."

To strengthen the brand further, in 2013 Shriver appointed its first public relations agency, Y&R, which will launch a new global integrated campaign including TV, print, digital, social media, youth activation and leadership, fundraising and global events. As he explains:

> We are ready for the world to engage with our brand, especially as we move towards the Special Olympics World Summer Games that will take place in Los Angeles 25 July – 2 August 2015. Most importantly, we are now poised to mobilize today's youth to break down even more barriers, enabling people of all ages in communities around the world to live, speak and play in a unified manner.

Shriver has also expanded the brand through programs in athlete leadership, cross-cultural research, health, education, and family support. Special Olympics Healthy Athletes® has become the world's largest public health screening and education program for people with intellectual disabilities. He has also campaigned for legislative and government support for issues of concern to the Special Olympics community, testifying before Congress on a few occasions. In 2000, he collaborated with Disney Studios to release a feature film about the Special Olympic athlete Loretta Claiborne. Claiborne was born with intellectual disabilities and partially blind, and was raised by a single mother of seven children. Her CV includes two honorary doctorate degrees, from Quinnipiac University in 1995 and Villanova University in 2003; 26 marathons with her best time 3:03, finishing in the top 100 women of the Boston Marathon; a 4th degree black belt in karate; skills in four languages and fluency in American Sign Language; public addresses to hundreds of groups including the US Congress, and two appearances on the Oprah Show. She has also carried the torch in the Special Olympics, has won medals in dozens of its events, and also held the women's record in her age group for the 5000 meters at 17 minutes. She credits Janet McFarland, a social worker who first introduced her to the Special Olympics, and founder Eunice Kennedy Shriver – alongside her own spirituality – for helping her develop the confidence to become a world-class runner. But the most rewarding part of her life, she says, has been her involvement with the Special Olympics, recognizing her potential to help others embrace life. "Find an opportunity and seize it", she says. "Be the best you can be, and never let anyone doubt you."[24]

In 2009, Smithsonian's National Portrait Gallery in Washington, DC unveiled the first portrait it has ever commissioned of an individual who has not served as President or First Lady. It was the portrait of Eunice Kennedy Shriver, and depicts her with four Special Olympics athletes including Loretta Claiborne.

3 Oprah

The message "Be the best you can be" is also at the heart of a very different brand: the one Oprah Winfrey established in her own name, beginning with the television show, but continuing far beyond it. She is the archetypal guide to life for the average American, and for women in particular, encouraging each member of her audience to achieve their dream. Television critics refer to her as everyone's best friend and yet also a spiritual leader of sorts. Her brand strapline? "Live your best life." Whether through the channel, the chat show or the magazine *O*, Oprah prompts people to raise their expectations of their own future.

In 2013, Winfrey came top of Forbes' list of the 100 most powerful global celebrities – based on earnings, media visibility, influence over social networks and marketability – for the fifth time, despite a fall in revenue of $88 million due to the close of her popular television talk show the year before.[25] Since, she has focused on building her OWN (for "Oprah Winfrey Network") cable media channel, a platform for live shows, videos and interactive discussion. OWN features Oprah's Lifeclass, a series of short videos and resources to help people address fundamental questions, such as finding your purpose in life, learning not to regret, or coming to terms with the absence of a father.

In the chat show, Winfrey would play a mirroring role, asking the questions, listening, prompting: "I don't get up every morning to come here and just have a little chatty talk", she insisted in a rare interview granted to a room of *O* readers, on the occasion of the magazine's tenth anniversary. "I have always been searching for how I can best be used."[26] Chat is never idle in the culture Oprah inspires: it's a medium for personal discovery, and one that Oprah facilitates by creating a safe space – albeit remarkably public – in which she encourages people to open up to her. Above all, she urges them to be true to themselves, "because that untruth blocks you from all you were meant to be".[27]

It works: people do open up. Famously, the actress Ellen DeGeneres spoke openly about her sexuality on the Oprah Winfrey Show in 1997, at a time when DeGeneres felt many would see her "as a freak".[28] De Generes recounts how, before the show, Madonna had sent her an inspiring quote, the words of an American modern dancer and choreographer, whose influence on dance has been compared to that of Picasso on the arts:

> There is a vitality, a life force, an energy, a quickening that is translated through you into action, and because there is only one of you in all

of time, this expression is unique. And if you block it, it will never exist through any other medium and it will be lost. The world will not have it.[29]

De Generes chose Oprah's show to release this vitality, in a moment that, according to one BBC journalist, not only underlined "Winfrey's reputation as confidante-in-chief, [but] also relaunched the career of DeGeneres, who went on to host her own chat show".[30]

Winfrey is in no doubt about the value of shared stories: the contagious nature of vitality, and the difference a positive precedent, or role model, can make. In June 2013, she donated $12 million towards the new museum of African American history in Washington DC, remarking: "I am deeply appreciative of those who paved the path for me and all who follow in their footsteps. By investing in this museum, I want to help ensure that we both honor and preserve our culture and history, so that the stories of who we are will live on for generations to come."[31]

Fifteen years before, in 1998, she had founded the philanthropic non-profit Oprah's Angel Network to encourage people around the world to create opportunities for other women and children to rise to their potential. In collaboration with Free The Children, Oprah's Angel Network has built over 55 schools in rural areas in 12 countries; and in 2007, the same collaborators launched O Ambassadors, a school-based program to inspire young people to become active, compassionate and knowledgeable global citizens. In 2000, the Network introduced the "Use Your Life Award" to celebrate the work of other philanthropic organizations.[32]

Of course, Winfrey's own vitality is the strongest card the brand has to play. In the future, brand Oprah will face growing competition from other inspirational personalities – who can easily be found on TED and YouTube. The potential of a personality to inspire doesn't necessarily depend on their active presence: more young entrepreneurs and digital enthusiasts are taking Steve Jobs as their role model following his death in 2011 than perhaps did before. Many of them have also spotted an appetite for personal development among consumers, responding with sites like The School of Life, which offers tools for thinking, and apps like Headspace, which teaches meditation through your mobile. Other women are coming forward to build empowering communities, too, such as Servane

Mouazan, founder of Oguntê, a network for women in social enterprise, and the Women's Social Leadership Awards.

Beyond Winfrey herself, is there a future for the brand? Quite possibly. Its strength is that Winfrey has always paid more attention to what other people say, and to the nuggets of energy she can unleash in them, than to herself. Her audience may regard her as a guru or guide: she sees herself as a prompt and facilitator.

5 Purpose

The desire for purpose is a creative impulse: through our will and our imagination, we take the things we do and say and give them meaning. Like an artist making a beautiful mosaic out of chips of broken pottery, we imagine what we'd like our days to add up to, and begin to structure them to that end. Why we do this, and whether or not we need to, has kept many a philosophers' café buzzing with debate. People do many things without purpose and, as we saw in Chapter Two, there can be lots to gain from motiveless adventure. They set off without any particular aim to pursue: they simply enjoy being on the road, the changing scenery and the potential to grow as a person thanks to the many unexpected outcomes of their openness to the world. If there are such rewards in approaching life without a particular aim in mind, why impose one, deciding how the story should end before you begin? In what way does a purpose enhance a life? The answer will always be particular to a person: their values, sociocultural context and, for many, their spiritual beliefs – but here are some general observations.

Moving – or even remaining and simply "being" – for any length of time without purpose is actually very difficult. Many people will have experienced the tedium of performing a job they find unrewarding. Chip Conley, Founder of Joie de Vivre (JDV) Hotels and author of the bestseller *Emotional Equations*, says there is a "high spiritual price for being more focused on means than meaning". You may make money, but to invest in which future? You may have status and power, but what is it you wish to influence? Conley talks of the despair that results from such situations with no exaggeration. He recounts that five of his friends and colleagues have committed suicide due to work-related stress. He summarizes his understanding as to why in one of the equations in his book: "Despair = Suffering − Meaning".

Many philosophers have looked to rise above this suffering. The Stoics sought to do this through acceptance, following a path defined by reason and virtue, but not directed by the will. Similarly, Buddhists strive to achieve a state of enduring satisfaction, in which existence is accepted on its own terms and all experiences welcomed as equal; the appropriate response to life is set out in the Noble Eightfold Path towards enlightenment − known as the Way of the Elders, or *Theravada* − which builds on the foundation of "right knowledge".

The French-Algerian writer Albert Camus discussed whether it is possible to overcome suffering by recognizing the meaningless of life, and embracing it. He was interested in how people can respond to what he described as the "Absurd": the paradoxical feeling that your life is important, but that it is also without meaning − and therefore has no value. He suggests that the logical response to this paradox is either to create meaning, which requires a leap of faith or double bluff, or to kill oneself. But, he later argues, attempting to defy logic, it is possible to value life, recognize that it is without meaning, and yet be happy. To illustrate this, he takes the Greek myth of Sisyphus, who is condemned by the gods to push a rock up a hill, follow it as it rolls back down to the plains, and push it back up again − for eternity. Camus imagines Sisyphus happy, because as he walks down the hill he resolves to strive on without hope of success, choosing to turn his punishment into his own purpose, drawing on the sheer force of his own will.

Politics and privilege

It is important to acknowledge that the freedom to choose a purpose is by no means a given. Sometimes people act with purpose but without personal conviction or desire. They perhaps are compelled: carrying out orders over which they have no choice. Or they are coerced: they *feel* they have no choice, placing enough value on a particular end – such as acceptance within a particular social context – to pursue it at whatever cost. Instances are prevalent, across the world: in the UK, asylum seekers, who do not have the right to seek employment, can come under pressure to work in unacceptable conditions, or to sell drugs or sex, in order to feed themselves or their family; by contrast, professionals earning a good wage can come under pressure to work long hours to the detriment of their health and family life, or to cut corners – such as safety standards – in order to boost profit margins.

Even within contexts of coercion and discrimination, people with conviction and courage find ways to pursue their purpose. They take a stand through protest, art and commentary, often devising ingenious ways to spread a message through underground or alternative media, frequently risking their lives. In Soviet Russia, the poet Yevgeny Yevtushenko disseminated his most famous poem, *Babiyy Yar* – written in 1961 to expose the Soviet Government's own persecution of the Jewish people and denounce its distortion of its role in the 1941 massacre at Babiyy Yar, in which 33,771 men, women and children were killed – in the underground samizdat press. Half a century later, in 2011, the Russian feminist punk rock group Pussy Riot sought to overcome the state's opposition to its pro-LGBT lyrics by wearing brightly colored balaclavas and using nicknames during interviews. Nonetheless, in 2012, three of the women were arrested, and two were sent to prison. A sense of moral justice and solidarity brings millions of people onto the streets each year in political demonstrations. They are led by both a generous instinct and by an acknowledgement of interdependence: that whatever threatens the lives and rights of others also destabilizes our own.

For those with the privilege of freedom, the desire to live with purpose can be strengthened by acknowledgement of their good fortune. Consider the commitment of children to their studies in contexts where schooling is neither readily available nor assumed to be a right. Even in the workplace, the liberty to decide upon something to strive for, and hone each decision with that end in mind, can be reserved for a few senior managers, or a privilege won through constant proof of commitment to someone else's purpose.

The value of a goal

A goal is an embodiment of purpose: a symbol for it and a communications tool of sorts. It offers a shortcut to a common understanding of the value of doing something. In sport, the goal is often the most prominent representation of the athletes' purpose. It has meaning because there is consensus about its qualities – its size or height, the distance of the course, or the number of hurdles. It has value because it is widely recognized – by the spectators, the referee and by the individual or team working towards it.

Working towards any goal demands some conviction about its worth. You need to have faith that, when you reach it, any promised rewards will indeed be there. When this faith is undermined, the impact on a person's motivation can be severe. Think of the anger of football players and supporters when a referee makes a call that is widely deemed unfair, or the disappointment of students when an examination board comes under fire for unreliable marking processes. When the goal stands on shaky ground, the efforts of everyone aiming for it are rendered meaningless.

A brand can make a goal worth aiming for by vouching for its value. There's little glory in the pedestal itself: it's just a few blocks in a stadium. But the crowds go wild when someone stands on it because a sporting body – be it the International Olympic Committee or the Association of Tennis Professionals – has made that person jump through many hoops, and is willing to vouch that they haven't cheated on the way.

A shared purpose

Finding a purpose means looking beyond any ready-made goals. You have to ask yourself what it is that matters to you and what you want to achieve, imagine what the outcome will look like and working out a path towards it. An athlete without a long-term purpose might feel low after they have achieved a goal: they may not be sure where to focus their energy next. If they have a long-term purpose – to help others enjoy sport, or improve access to facilities – they'll already be looking to their next steps.

Finding a purpose means looking beyond any ready-made goals

Many people find purpose by working in solidarity with others, and more brands are moving in this direction. "Corporate social responsibility" has become a staple chapter in many annual reports, although too often it is a disappointing add-on, a bit of charity on the side, rather than part and parcel of the company's core mission and operations. Others make the creation of lasting value their mission.

Take the International Olympic Committee, for instance. Creating a successful event is only part of what it sets out to do. It also aims to lay the foundations and infrastructure for thriving communities in host cities, to encourage a new generation of athletes, and to raise the bar for the management and procurement practice of future global events. Among its claims for the legacy of London 2012 are ten railway lines and 30 new bridges connecting communities after the Game, and a ten-year ecological management plan to encourage biodiversity in 45 hectares of habitat. It also claims that the London 2012 Games raised standards for sustainable construction, with a focus on recycling and repurposing material that would no longer be needed after the event. As part of this, a partnership between DOW Chemical, the development charity Article 25 and Axion Recycling was set up to repurpose parts of the stadium for social projects in the UK, as well as for shelter solutions in Uganda and Rio.[1]

Actions that are motivated by a long-term purpose, or that have the interests of other people at heart, can also bring benefits to the person or organization behind them. More and more companies are investing in their supply chains, with risk management in mind. For instance, Nestlé's Cocoa Plan provided training to 27,000 farmers in 2012, with the aim of improving their practices and boosting their yields – in quality as well as volume. It offers advice on pruning so that trees don't get too tall, so saving time when it comes to harvesting, how to dry cocoa beans to minimize spoilage, and how to manage pests while reducing the need for pesticides. It is also partnering with the Fair Labor Association to eliminate child labor in cocoa farms, and working with the World Cocoa Foundation to build or refurbish 40 schools in the Cote d'Ivoire by 2016. This is all sound business practice: Nestlé's investment will enhance long-term profitability by ensuring that there are healthy crops in years to come, and by looking after the next generation of farmers. "Without farmers, there'd be no cocoa", runs the logic, and "without cocoa, there'd be no chocolate."[2]

There is nothing sneaky about what Nestlé calls "shared value". We all depend on shared resources, and so there is little lasting value (if any) in benefits that only one person gets to enjoy. However, trust is eroded when practices with self-interest at heart masquerade as philanthropy. It's a question that recurs on the global stage: foreign interventions are often presented to the public with a discourse based on empathy, moral conviction and social justice thinly veiling the pursuit of domestic interests. When it comes to natural resources, our interest could be accompanied by a sense of our dependence on ecosystems that will malfunction if mistreated, inspiring people to live in a way that will enable these to thrive when they are long gone. On the other hand, that interest may be purely motivated by the short-term potential of land, water, forest and fuel to enhance one's own wealth.

CHALLENGE YOUR BRAND

- Is there anything preventing your brand or your audience from pursuing a purpose?
- How is your brand creating shared value?
- In what way could investment in other people benefit your brand?

Unleashing the imagination

Theodore Levitt – the influential Harvard economist and proponent of differentiation mentioned in the Introduction – spoke of the importance of the imagination as an engine that drives us towards a goal. "The idea precedes the deed", he said. Levitt was particularly interested in creating purpose within a commercial context:

> Imagination means to construct mental pictures of what is or is not actually present, what has never been actually experienced. To exercise the imagination is to be creative. It requires intellectual or artistic inventiveness. Anybody can do it, and most people often do – unfortunately, however, only in daydreams and fantasies, when they are not constrained by convention or conviction. To do it in business requires shedding these constraints but also discipline, especially the discipline of dissociation from what exists and what has been.

Today, the buzzword for change-makers the world over is innovation. For Levitt, it was progress. The notion of progress ties purpose into a long string of events. It assumes that each knot in the string builds on the previous one, in a seemingly straight line. This is a narrowing of perspective, not an opening of the mind. If you are only looking to do more of what has been done before, you might miss a great left-of-field opportunity.

Sometimes what looks like progress to one person could look like a step backwards to another. A radical new business model can mean any number of things: for the entrepreneur it might mean a step towards prosperity; for an established brand it might mean new competition; or it might play a part in the destabilization of a whole system. The outcome might be so different from the original market that there is no comparison to make.

Broken systems sometimes need to be overturned in order to establish healthier ones in their place. This is the mission of the global non-profit Forum for the Future. It brings together various organizations and people with interests in common, and helps them to imagine various versions of the future, and to plot a course towards the most resilient and desirable possibilities. For instance, it convened the Sustainable Shipping Initiative, bringing together some of the biggest names in the maritime industry – including Maersk and Cargill – to imagine the challenges they will face in 2040 and decide on a common course of action.

Progress also assumes a lasting impact, but sometimes a strong sense of purpose can lead us to do things whose value is in the moment. Think of the current trend for pop-up shops. When they "pop down" again, they haven't failed. What they may have done is to bring a sense of potential back into moribund high streets, and left a space for others to dream up new purposes.

Levitt was very clear about the object of establishing a purpose, and applied his thinking to marketers. The object for them, he said, is "to get and keep a customer, and also to get existing buyers to prefer to do business with you rather than your competitors". Now, with the dawn of Marketing 3.0 (Kotler's term for a new era in which marketers approach their audience as people, and not merely consumers – see Introduction), brand strategists must do more than "getting and keeping" customers: they need to find ways to engage with them as people with their own lives and purpose to pursue. The first question a brand needs to ask is, what do people imagine for their future? Then the brand needs to ask itself: what can it do to help?

> ## CHALLENGE YOUR BRAND
>
> – What does the future have in store for your brand?
> – Picture the people in your audience: what are they striving towards?
> – How can you inspire the people you reach to dream?

India: the rise of social purpose

India is the second most rapidly growing economy in the world. In 2012, the global advertising agency Edelman reported that citizens with spending power in India feel empowered to make a positive difference to society – and are looking to brands for support. The study found that "nearly four out of five Indians (79 per cent) want brands to make it easier for them to make a positive difference in the world". It also found that they look for the same social commitment from brands, asserting that "94 per cent of consumers in India believe it is important for businesses to have a social commitment". Globally, 31 per cent of consumers are aware of brands that place as much or more importance on supporting a good cause as they place on profits; in India, Edelman found, the proportion is much higher, at 58 per cent.[3]

Why should a newly empowered group of citizens look to brands for support, when it comes to issues of social justice? For a better understanding of spending power in this market, let's turn to the Indian economist Amartya Sen, winner of the 1998 Nobel Peace Prize. Sen sees economic development as a "process of expanding the real freedoms that people enjoy". His notion of freedom includes "being able to avoid such deprivations as starvation, under nourishment, escapable morbidity and premature mortality, as well as the freedoms that are associated with being literate and numerate, enjoying political participation and uncensored speech and so on".[4] Sen argues that freedom is not just an end – it is also the means to solving these social problems. "The instrumental role of freedom concerns the way different kinds of rights, opportunities and entitlements contribute to the expansion of human freedom in general, and thus to promoting development."[5] If Indian citizens perceive economic development in the same way – not as growth for growth's sake, as it is treated in many developed countries, but as a crucial means to social freedom, upon which any individual's ability to pursue a purpose depends – then the empowerment of people as consumers is but a milestone towards the higher goal of freedom for all.

India's growing middle class is also looking beyond its spending power to exert its influence – through political activism or grassroots organizations. The Edelman report notes that "the percentage of Indian consumers personally involved with social causes has significantly increased from 61 per cent in 2008 to 78 per cent in 2012, whereas the global total still remains at 55 per cent". It is interesting, therefore, that Indians are also demonstrating their belief in the potential of brands to have positive impacts on society – and an optimism that they will.

Sally Uren, CEO of Forum for the Future, which works with some of India's largest brands to solve difficult challenges, is not surprised:

> The reason this area is so full of optimism, is that brands give people control. Because who controls brands? We do! And that's an important thing to note. We can't control the climate really; we can't control when the next hurricane will hit, or the next flood. And we humans are wired in such a way that if we feel out of control we feel stressed. But we can control brands. Brands can just be a kind of extension of ourselves.

One brand that is responding to the pursuit of social purpose in India is Unilever's Lifebuoy, which sells soap and personal hygiene products. In 2010 it launched the Lifebuoy Handwashing Behavior Change program, with the aim to change the hygiene behavior of one billion people across Asia, Africa and Latin America by 2015 – in particular, by getting people to wash their hands with soap, targeting key occasions: before eating, after using the toilet and when washing. One of its main focuses is India, which, according to Unicef and the World Health Organization, has the highest number of children under five dying from diarrhoeal disease, with over 380,000 deaths a year, or more than 1000 a day.[6] In one campaign, Lifebuoy has stamped its message onto the first roti – an Indian flatbread eaten by hand – served with every meal at over 100 cafes and restaurants during Kumbh Mela. This mass Hindu pilgrimage attracts 100 million people every third year to bathe in one of India's four most sacred rivers. It is considered the largest peaceful gathering in the world, and attracts a unique crowd, predominantly from small towns and rural areas across India: the very people it is crucial Lifebuoy reaches. The words "Lifebuoy se haath dhoye kya?" ("Did you wash your hands with Lifebuoy?") were heat stamped onto the baked roti, leaving them completely edible. "The 'Roti Reminder' gets a consumer's attention at the exact time when handwashing is critical to help stop the spread of germs carrying preventable diseases", says Sudhir Sitapati, General Manager, Skin Cleansing at Hindustan Unilever Limited.[7] The brand's handwashing campaign is also targeting school children, new mothers, neo-natal nurses and community groups in Thesgora, a village with one of the highest rates of diarrhoea.

In 2013, Lifebuoy launched a three-minute film – watched by over 7 million in its first six months – on YouTube and Facebook to encourage people living in countries where clean water and low rates of child mortality can be taken for granted to empathize with the personal tragedy that results from the lack of infrastructure and education around basic hygiene. The film tells the story of a man, walking on his hands down the street, out of the village, through the fields, over gravel and through puddles, the sweat dripping from his forehead, followed by his son and a growing train of supporters and admirers, to a well where he finally sits down and is handed a chai. He raises his arms in celebration, saying that today is his son's fifth birthday. A passer-by asks what's so special about turning five and learns that this is the first child of his to reach that age.[8] The film closes with the statistics, and asks the viewer to "help every child reach its fifth birthday" in three ways: by making a pledge in support of handwashing on Facebook and allowing the campaign platform to post updates on the site on their behalf; by spreading the word, through sharing the film and following the hashtag #helpachildreach5 on Twitter; and by washing their own hands at key occasions and teaching children to do the same.

CHALLENGE YOUR BRAND

- How does your brand engage with people about social challenges?
- How can your brand support people to spend with purpose?
- Which everyday habits could your brand influence to improve lives?

Putting your money where your mouth is

Unilever has set out to rethink all of its brands, so that purpose is placed at the core of its mission and activities. I asked Marc Mathieu, Senior Vice President, Marketing at Unilever, about the rationale for doing this, and prompted him to describe his understanding of a brand's social purpose across global markets.

> We need to understand the purpose of a brand, not just on the product side, but also on the human side. Clearly, there is a unique opportunity within the parameter of brands to evolve, but there is also a necessity. More and more we're going to see people *not* buying a brand, because they don't trust the role that the brand plays in those larger social dimensions; if they think the brand is purely a commercial product, then they will penalize it. Only a small proportion will buy a brand because of its role in society, but more and more we'll see people who don't want to trade their money just for other people to become rich without having some kind of values system behind that.

With particular reference to Lifebuoy's video campaign, he explained that "the brand extends to me [the viewer] an opportunity to participate in creating meaning for myself, and doing it as part of a community on Facebook or on [other] social media means there's a bonding aspect, a social dimension: I defend something I care about."

The opportunities for individuals to express their purpose in society have expanded through social media. Pay rolls and job titles have long served as the primary means of recognizing an individual's role in society, regrettably encouraging many to gloss over the very significant economic contribution of parents, carers and domestic workers. The likes of Twitter, Facebook and LinkedIn offer more flexibility in how people respond on learning about issues they find important, integrating the public and private contexts of their lives. A video with the potential to go viral on social media creates an opportunity for a person to tell both colleagues and friends about an issue – and gives a brand an opportunity to discover what people care about. By tracking its progress, the brand can observe how certain ideas or stories inspire a sense of purpose. As people share their personal sense of purpose more frequently and more publicly than ever before, a brand that has nothing to contribute will quickly be relegated.

Moreover, by driving expressions of social purpose through these massive global online sharing platforms, a brand has the potential to bring together communities, uniting them through a common sense of purpose. Whereas the act of creating a purpose and deciding to pursue it must take place within each individual, there's strength and sway in numbers. The rationale for supporting a particular cause is understood through conversation with others; the significance of a cause is reinforced through the commitment of others; the sense of making a difference is enhanced by the response of others, and one's ability to do so is increased by the involvement of others. A brand campaign can therefore be a powerful way to enhance purpose.

In 2010, Unilever entered into a partnership with Carrotmob, an advocacy organization looking to enhance the power of consumer groups to influence brands. Carrotmob acts as a representative for people looking to spend their money in a purposeful way, and asks the business to make an improvement in return for their custom. "In a boycott, everyone loses. In a Carrotmob, everyone wins", the logic goes. The "mobbers" have the opportunity to assert their influence, while the brand gains new custom, increased sales (in the short term at least), the chance to involve its members in finding a solution to an issue they are concerned about, and promotion through Carrotmob's website and social media channels. For instance, in Rennes, France, a group of local purpose-led consumers ate and drank at three participating bars, and in return for their custom, these bars upgraded their lighting, captured wasted energy from heat, and changed their power supplier. In Mexico City, another group of "Carrotmobbers" flocked into Neveria Roxy ice-cream parlor, and in return the parlor improved its refrigeration, decreasing its power consumption by 30 per cent – a saving paid for through the immediate windfall, leaving the business to enjoy reduced energy bills in the long term. In Unilever's case, a Fresh & Easy store in Pasadena, California, agreed to invest in five non-ozone depleting freezers if 250 or more people took part in a sort of supermarket sweep-come-treasure hunt, in which they learned about the sustainability commitments of Ben & Jerry's ice cream, Ragu sauce and Skippy peanut butter – and were prompted to show their approval with their purse. During the day the sales volume of those products increased by 122 per cent.

As Uren observes:

> Paul Polman knows he needs to make a shed load of money to keep his investors happy. But I think he honestly believes – unless he's been

lying to everybody – that if you get the purpose right, the money will follow. Because the purpose will be speaking to real people. And I can buy that logic. Because if a business has a purpose that actually no one's that interested in, then you're not going to do very well at all.

CHALLENGE YOUR BRAND

- What media do members of your audience use to express their social purpose?
- If your brand was "Carrotmobbed", what would the campaigners ask for?
- What does your brand hope to change through its campaigns?

Knowledge is power

The key to a successful purpose-led campaign is that it offers a clear route to meaningful actions. Sharing a film or "liking" it on Facebook is a small action, a tiny goal for both the brand and the user. It is not a path to purpose unless it also asks for ongoing commitment to certain actions, and supports the person to follow them. However, the ideal campaign will support individuals to develop their own strategies, applying their minds and creativity to solving problems. This way, the campaign stops being something the brand owns and the individual merely nods at, and becomes a shared effort – a purpose to which every person can apply their particular knowledge and skills.

A first step towards this is to offer educational resources, helping people to get a clearer grip on the issues, their root causes, and what needs to be done about them. This can transform the anger and frustration that can often accompany strong feelings of injustice, or a feeling of powerlessness, into an informed response and a way forward. For instance, Lifebuoy's "Help a child reach 5" campaign offers an online health map, where you can find out about local health alerts around the world, tracking the incidence of infectious diseases by date (with daily updates) or by global location.[9] At a glance, you can learn that on 14 August 2013, 20 students of a city school in Maharashtra, India, fell ill with gastroenteritis after eating chocolate to celebrate a classmate's birthday, with a link to the news release.[10] Disappointingly, the Press Trust of India reports that the school subsequently banned birthday celebrations involving chocolates, asking the students to share written messages instead: the handwashing message has some way to go. Accompanying the interactive map is a series of top tips targeting parents of schoolchildren, to help them keep infections at bay: washing hands with soap is top of the list, followed by the importance of healthy habits, eating well, spending time out of doors, as infections are commonly transmitted in closed environments, and so on. You can also read about specific infections, learning about their causes, prevention and treatment.

A better understanding of a problem increases the potential for a person to develop their own response to it. But education has a broader scope than the acquisition of knowledge. If brands can support people to develop skills in critical analysis of the world around them, they will be able to identify their own cause to support, prompting a whole societal shift towards purposeful living. You may well be thinking that this sounds too "worthy" to be a likely brand strategy – but there are successful precedents.

"Brands have been convenors of significant social change in the past", Uren asserts. "They can be agents, not just for transformation in the sense of behavior change, but they can shift societal norms. If you look at Port Sunlight, they helped the whole community in the north-west of England develop." Port Sunlight is a suburb of Wirral in Merseyside, which Lever Brothers started building in 1888 to offer accommodation to workers in its new soap factory; both the factory and houses were built on unused marshy land close to both the River Mersey and a railway line. William Lever's declared aim was "to socialise [sic] and Christianise [sic] business relations and get back to that close family brotherhood" – sharing profits through investment in the neighborhood. They built 800 homes with gardens, allotments, an art gallery, a concert hall, a hospital, an open-air swimming pool, a church and a temperance hotel (a place to relax without drinking) – and then offered educational programs and encouraged organizations to promote art, literature, science and music. The town became a celebrated site of creativity: it was the subject of a West End show in 1912, and the concert hall was the venue for Ringo Starr's debut with The Beatles.[11]

Epiphanies and purpose

William Lever attributed his own sense of social purpose to his Christian faith. He didn't set out as a missionary, though, instead focusing on the creation of jobs, education and the development of strong communities within healthy contexts: a foundation for purposeful lives.

Similarly, George Cadbury set up a business selling tea, coffee and cocoa in response to his values as a Quaker, seeking to promote alternatives to alcohol. The Quakers (or the Religious Society of Friends – a group with Christian roots that began in England in the 1650s) do not have a defined creed or set of beliefs, and so there is no "ban" as such on alcohol consumption; rather, they are concerned with an individual's freedom of conscience and ability to develop their own beliefs, letting that light guide them as a person.[12]

Many successful business leaders describe the moment at which their values appeared to them in a stronger light, giving them a new insight into the world through which they developed a clearer understanding of their role in it – their purpose. Take the late Ray Anderson, the Founder and Chairman of Interface, who was awarded eleven honorary doctorates, and honored by many prestigious institutions, including the Harvard Business School, the Institute for Business and Professional Ethics, and the World Business Academy. Anderson founded the company which introduced the carpet tile to America in 1973. Over 20 years later, he read Paul Hawken's book *The Ecology of Commerce*, and experienced his epiphany: "I wasn't halfway through it before the vision I sought became clear, along with a powerful sense of urgency to do something." Anderson famously described Hawken's message as a spear in his chest. In his words, Hawken "charges business and industry as, one, the major culprit in causing the decline of the biosphere, and, two, the only institution that is large enough, and pervasive enough, and powerful enough, to really lead humankind out of this mess".

Anderson's vision was to transform his petroleum-intensive carpet company so that it would "take from the earth only what could be renewed by the earth rapidly and naturally, and to do no harm to the biosphere". By leading his company towards this goal, he hoped to "lead the entire industrial world". He later read Daniel Quinn's *Ishmael*, which he says compounded his sense of purpose. He was struck by Quinn's metaphor of early attempts at building aircraft, in which "pedal-powered airplane men" tried to fly without understanding the laws of aerodynamics, sending their planes "off high cliffs for the sensation of flying, only to crash to the ground."[13] For Anderson, the cliff represents the seemingly unlimited resources the civilization can draw upon: the fall illustrates the consequence of plundering them. Learning to fly means understanding what resources a business depends on, and investing in them. He set about transforming Interface's mission, beginning with a detailed analysis of all the energy and raw materials that went into its production systems.

Jonathon Porritt, the Founder-Director of Forum for the Future, wrote a tribute to Anderson following his death in August 2011. He observed that what made Ray Anderson stand out as a leader was his pursuit of knowledge: "Ray didn't just read, he hunted it down. Having discovered The Natural Step (TNS), which remains the most rigorous of all the different models for understanding sustainability, he insisted on nailing it down to the last detail." This knowledge, says Porritt, brought responsibility – which is one of the strongest foundations for purpose: a respect for the resources on which creative energy thrives. Anderson then sought to nurture the same understanding in all of his employees, putting every single one through a basic TNS training course, so that they would all have the opportunity to pursue their jobs with a sense of purpose.

CHALLENGE YOUR BRAND

- Have you had an epiphany? How did it change your work?
- What resources could your brand offer to inspire people to think about their purpose?
- To what extent do you identify with your brand's purpose? How engaged are your colleagues?

How purpose drives performance

"People who find their reason for being, who uncover their purpose and connect with it passionately, become more engaged and significantly more effective at work and in life because of a clear sense of fulfillment", writes Shawn Parr, CEO of the San Diego-based innovation and design company Bulldog Drummond, in *Fast Company* magazine.[14] It sounds like common sense, but what evidence is there? A study by the Institute for Corporate Policy found that 71 per cent of high-performing organizations said that actively promoting performance management by creating a connection with the corporate mission was critical to their success.[15] The

2013 Deloitte Core Beliefs and Culture Survey found that "organizations that focus beyond profits and create 'a culture of purpose' are more likely to find long-term success". The survey also found that 91 per cent of respondents who said their company has a strong sense of purpose also said it has a history of strong financial performance. It identified activities that contribute to creating a sense of purpose at work, such as products and services that make a positive impact on clients, employee development and mentorship, and volunteerism. Punit Renjen, Chairman of the Board at Deloitte LLP, observed, "Many businesses have made great strides to strengthen their role as corporate citizens. However, our survey suggests that there is still so much more work to do". Companies that continue to develop their social role, defining their purpose and working towards it, could see a positive impact on their performance in the long term, Renjen adds.[16]

One reason purpose enhances performance is that it feels good. This is clear in the passion with which people talk about their mission – Ray Anderson is one example, and this book is packed with comments from other passionate professionals. It's also clear in the tenacity with which people pursue their purpose – and Chip Conley of JDV found this applies at all levels of an organization, even among the people cleaning the toilets in his hotels.

Abraham Maslow put purpose at the very top of his hierarchy of needs, as part of self-actualization. On the one hand, this position implies his assertion that we can only really find meaning in life once other needs, those he saw as more basic, have been satisfied – such as a wage to pay for food and shelter; but if every person were first to build their home and stock the fridge (leaving the questions of interior design and taste for later) before they began to look for purpose, they might find they come to it rather late, and after many years of dissatisfaction. Conley took away another lesson when he revisited Maslow in 2001. He was concerned JDV would go bankrupt during the second economic downturn that the San Francisco Bay area had experienced in ten years, and was looking for inspiration. He noted that self-actualization sits at the top of the hierarchy because that is where Maslow placed an individual's deepest motivations: those that "take on an inspirational quality". Conley was struck that when Maslow interviewed nurses, asking them about their relationship with their work, and why they went into nursing, "the nurses answered by describing peak experiences that were virtually life-altering. Nurses who were most able to express a peak experience seemed most 'called' by their work."[17] Conley concludes that the nurses' passion enables them to "transcend the bartering relationship" in which employees give their time and skills in return for money and recognition. Instead, these nurses "have tapped into an internal motivation that fuels them. They are inspired by what they do. They have moved from just focusing on the tasks they do each day to imagining the impact of their work".

Conley sought to apply this to his own company. He had called it "Joie de Vivre" in the first place because he wanted its mission to be its brand – but he felt his employees were perhaps losing sight of the aim, that they weren't feeling their calling. He took to asking them questions in monthly meetings, such as, "What's the best experience you've had in the past month here at work?", or prompting them to ask themselves, "What am I becoming as a result of this job?" Alongside these questions, he also set about creating a more democratic culture, calling on employees to help define the business strategy. As a result, he claims, JDV's turnover rate dropped to one-third the industry average, and was crowned the second best place to work in the San Francisco Bay Area – "a remarkable feat for a service company that's full of people cleaning toilets in a region full of high-tech companies famous for plush corporate campuses."

He has a point. Cleaning toilets is not many people's idea of a meaningful job – but that would be missing the point. Cleaning toilets or making a bed is a short-term goal that sits under JDV's "umbrella" purpose of offering people a space in which to appreciate life. Conley distinguishes between meaning at work and meaning in work, and argues that "at work" is more important. Nonetheless, he is aware that merely believing in the brand mission isn't enough: you need to see how your role contributes to it, and you need to have the capacity to influence it. With a hand in the toilet, you might be much closer to spotting efficiencies in water use – or the difference a really well-scented soap would make to a guest – than your manager upstairs.

Does management get in the way?

The Quakers reject priests and rituals as an unnecessary obstruction between the believer and God. Should businesses do away with managers and performance reviews as an unnecessary obstruction between the employee and their purpose? It's a theory growing in popularity, with some pioneers moving away from hierarchical business structures altogether.

One organization to renounce hierarchy in the hope of getting even closer to purpose is The Otesha Project UK – a spin-off from the Canadian youth-led non-profit organization, whose name is a Swahili word meaning "reason to dream". Otesha UK has transitioned from having one executive director to a team of five co-directors, alongside "decently paid interns who have an equal say but don't take on any managerial or administrative responsibility". Its founder and now co-director, Liz McDowell, observes that the shift has placed a much greater emphasis on learning – which, as we have seen, is a crucial foundation for creative thinking about the future, and what any one individual or organization can contribute. She explains that every team member needs to understand all aspects of the organization's methods – from its finances to its legal structure "and everything in between" – in order to make informed decisions in their own roles. The new democratic structure allows everyone, she argues, "ownership not just of their own silo but of Otesha as a whole".[18] In this context, the term "ownership" implies more than the transactional arrangement that makes a person with a job description responsible for a particular task: it implies the freedom to align the role with one's own values.

This is the whole point, or purpose, of Otesha: to offer training and resources to young people so that they can "connect [their] day-to-day choices with their global impacts". Alongside resources to help people reconsider their lifestyle habits, such as how they eat, shop and travel, through a lens of social and environmental purpose, Otesha runs programs to help 16-25-year-olds in East London find meaningful work. Its Brand Out program focuses on the horticultural sector, offering free training in practical skills, accredited by City & Guilds, as well as a mentor to encourage reflection, support to find employment, and even cooking classes and money management skills, in collaboration with Made in Hackney and Mybank.

The organization asserts that freedom and choice are key to its purpose-enhancing mission, and works to challenge and remove "oppression caused by power inequalities in society, both systemic and on an individual level". An explanation of its anti-oppression stance refers to the work of the

Canadian social work theorist Bob Mullaly, author of the book *Challenging Oppression and Confronting Privilege*. As Mullaly writes:

> [H]ierarchies of power and privilege are embedded in our culture and social institutions in a way that is often invisible. They affect how we see the world and how we work together. They also limit our capacity to make positive change, since freedom from oppression is one of the necessary building blocks for a just and responsible society.

This idea – that one person's freedom depends on another's – is reinforced through a well-known saying, attributed to Lilla Watson, a Murri visual artist, activist and academic: "If you have come here to help me, then you are wasting your time. But if you have come because your liberation is bound up with mine, then let us work together."[19]

How freedom fuels innovation

A flat structure is all very well for a small non-profit, you may well be thinking, but what about a commercial brand? How could an SME achieve its mission and maintain its financial performance with no official management structure – let alone a multinational? Valve, a Washington-based technology company founded in 1996 and which now employs 300 people, was set up not only without management structure but with no job titles or defined roles at all, on the conviction that this structure was the best way to achieve its high-growth mission. Its founder, Gabe Newell, had been working at Microsoft and went to visit the software company Id, the company responsible for the creation of the computer game *Doom*, which had reached more personal computers than the world's largest software company. Id was then a company of ten people in their twenties, based in Mesquite, Texas – as one of Newell's colleagues, Michael Abrash, tells the story in a blog.[20] Newell surmised that "something fundamental had changed about the nature of productivity". He looked into the history of hierarchical management and found that it had been invented for military purposes, "where it was perfectly suited to getting 1000 men to march over a hill to get shot at". He could see how this made sense during the industrial revolution, in which each person was expected to act as a component in a machine, doing the same tasks over and over again. He saw that this was no longer the case: that "almost all the value was in performing a valuable creative act for the first time". For a software company to be successful in a highly competitive market, it would need to innovate at every opportunity, and never to repeat itself. In the hope of giving his employees the best chance of achieving this, Newell set up Valve with as much freedom and as little structure as possible. As well as no job descriptions, there are no set working hours, no managers and no performance reviews. All the projects are self-directed. If roles are allocated within a project, they are agreed by consensus and are temporary. New employees are given a handbook to set them off on "a fearless adventure in knowing what to do when no one's there telling you". It explains the rationale:

> A flat structure removes every organizational barrier between your work and the customer enjoying that work. Every company will tell you that "the customer is boss," but here that statement has weight. There's no red tape stopping you from figuring out for yourself what our customers want, and then giving it to them.[21]

The company interacts with its users by inviting them into its studios to test the games, and listening to feedback on digital forums. I did ask Abrash, who is currently working on wearable software, whether any of Valve's products had an aim similar to the company's management approach – to unleash creative risk-taking – he said he hadn't ever thought about it. A missed opportunity?

CHALLENGE YOUR BRAND

- How free are you to pursue your purpose at work?
- Does your management ever get in the way of innovation?
- How could your brand experiment with hierarchy?

The pitfalls of packaging purpose

Work isn't the only place where people find purpose. But for any brand seeking to package it up for a wider audience, it's an important place to start: put your own house in order first, as the adage goes. If your own actions don't make sense to you, it will be difficult to inspire others with the necessary conviction to give their actions a strong shape. Moreover, there are the potential rewards in terms of productivity, financial returns and opportunities for innovation, and also the fact that a brand's employees are as much part of its audience as anyone in the general public – and even more likely to advocate its life-enhancing purpose, if only through exposure to it. You can take a safe bet that no one at Valve asked Abrash to write a great blog, on a microsite he created himself, telling the world about the ideas behind his company's management structure. He simply had the freedom to share an approach that he had found valuable on a personal level: one that had helped him to pursue an outcome of his choosing, playing roles he found interesting and through which he could develop his own skills.

Brands that package purpose for their commercial audience without really making it their central concern risk criticism for the resulting disconnect between their claims and the reality of the experience. Take voluntourism, a growing industry that offers an alternative to idle repose in exotic locations, through short-term volunteering projects in disadvantaged communities – often advertising the opportunity as a more authentic overseas experience and charging a considerable fee for it. An estimated 10 million travellers now participate in such projects each year, according to the travel association ABTA. Not all such packages are alike, though. The distinguishing factor is, of course, the purpose of the organizing brand, and the extent to which this purpose is shaped by extensive interaction with the community in question. A project well-managed can bring both manpower and financial support to solve problems identified by the local community, helping to implement their own solutions. On the other hand, poorly managed projects can deprive locals of jobs by bringing in free labor and, in the worst cases, perpetuate the problem for the sake of continuing the voluntourism program.

For instance, the Alternative Spring Break (ASB) is a week-long package for college students organized by Western University. The website carries the following endorsement: "It immerses you in a different world, it challenges you in the most meaningful ways, and it can inspire and direct you for the rest of your life into living a life of meaning and fulfillment". However, Ossob Mohamud describes his own experience as an ASB participant in a blog on the Guardian Africa Network:

> Interspersed throughout the week were touristy getaways and souvenir shopping. Although I had memorable and rewarding moments, I could

never shake off the feeling that it was all a bit too self-congratulatory and disingenuous.

Mohamud goes on to explain that by entering into these communities with little or no understanding of the locals' history, culture and ways of life, all the student is able to observe is:

> ...the poverty and the presumed neediness of the community... leading to condescending and superficial relationships that transform the (usually Western) volunteer into a benevolent giver and the community members into the ever grateful receivers of charity.

He questions whether the trips are designed more for the volunteers' spiritual fulfillment than for the community itself. In any case, Mohamud certainly did not come away with a feeling of fulfillment. Worse still, he believes the volunteers slowed down the process of building houses, due to their "inexperience and clumsiness". He asks whether the volunteers would not spend their time better campaigning for IMF and World Bank reforms, or advocating for their home country to change aggressive foreign policies.

Real Gap Experience and i-to-i are among a number of operators working with the travel association ABTA to develop new guidelines for sustainable voluntourism, reports Ben Goldfarb in *Green Futures* magazine. Matt Fenton, Product Manager at Real Gap Experience, admits that regular interaction with the community is crucial. Real Gap works with partner organizations in the host community:

> Before we embark on a partnership, we discuss with them what tangible, long-term outcomes they're looking to achieve [in order] to ensure a positive benefit for all. We're constantly getting feedback from communities about what's happening on the ground.[22]

Saga is another ABTA member that seeks to ensure that the purpose of the local community is at the heart of its projects. Saga's volunteers are all aged 50 or over, and the organizers spend time matching their individual experiences and qualifications to the needs of the project, and ensuring that one volunteer is able to pick up where another left off, in order to deliver "genuine lasting benefit". The projects have the final say in whether a volunteer is suitable, and can decide what role they should play.

Desire-led brands in action

Let's take a brisk tour through the many ways in which a brand can respond to the desire for purpose. We began with Nestlé, which has an eye on the long-term needs of its supply chain. It recognizes that it depends on the present and future wellbeing of its cocoa farmers, and so is supporting them to think about their future too, offering training for the farmers and education for their children.

Brands can work with people to create visions of their lives or their industry in years to come. Forum for the Future is doing this with the whole shipping sector; Otesha is working with young people one on one. Both organizations prompt people to ask, "What sort of world would I like to live in?" and "How can I bring it about?"

Purpose doesn't come from thin air: even people with a great imagination draw on a wide range of resources to inspire them. Just as Ray Anderson supported his staff to read and to learn, a brand can bring together resources and inspire people by curating this information in stimulating ways.

A brand can also share its vision with the wider world. Lifebuoy's "Help a child reach 5" campaign offers a clear set of actions to help people work towards it, beginning with washing your hands – a small but very important goal towards the higher purpose of reducing child mortality.

Finally, a brand can choose either to assign roles – the approach of Real Gap, working with the host community to ensure the visiting voluntourists have a positive impact – or push people to create a role for themselves, like Valve.

In the following section, I explore how three brands have identified and interpreted the desire of people in particular contexts to develop their own purpose in life, and the role they have established to support them. Here are some key questions to consider:

- How is this brand working with people to develop their sense of purpose?
- How is it helping to remove barriers to purpose?
- What resources does it offer to inspire people to apply themselves in new ways?

Case studies

1   Grameen Bank

In the last half-century, few people have presented such a challenge to the purpose of business in society as the economics professor Muhammad Yunus, who founded Grameen Bank on the principle that if you lend them money, people will solve their own problems. Yunus observed that, prior to Grameen Bank, organizations seemed to operate in only one of two ways: either they aimed to benefit their owners by making a profit or they aimed to benefit other people through government-led social programs or charity. He saw a gap in the market for "social businesses", whose primary purpose would be to address society's needs. To nurture such an approach, he realized, entrepreneurs without any other access to credit would need loans based on trust and accountability. Such a loan would also offer them a way into meaningful social participation through the freedom to apply their own creativity to improve their lives. Yunus believed in the power of individual purpose, arguing that "these millions of small people with their millions of small pursuits can add up to create the biggest development wonder". When he set out the seven principles of social business, he began with the purpose of the enterprise, and concluded with the joy of the person pursuing it.[23] He had no doubt that people would jump at the opportunity to give their lives structure and meaning.

In 1976, he founded the Grameen (which means "rural" in Bangla) Bank Project to offer credit to the rural poor of Bangladesh, and 30 years later both the founder and the bank were awarded the 2006 Nobel Peace Prize for their contribution towards economic and social development, democracy, human rights and lasting peace. The Norwegian Nobel Committee declared that Grameen Bank had been a source of ideas and models for the many institutions in the field of micro-credit that have sprung up around the world. It still is. Recent additions to the scene of microfinance and incubators for social enterprise include London Creative Labs, Youth Finance International, based in Amsterdam, and Kiva, a US-based crowd-sourcing platform which allows any member of the public to make a loan to an entrepreneur and to watch their business grow, through email updates.

Today, Grameen is pursuing partnerships with educational institutions, to encourage more young people to consider their purpose in society.

In a report released in 2013, it argued that "more than ever before", universities have an important role to play in encouraging social business. They offer "a breeding ground for knowledge and new ideas", but also a critical environment in which people can question dominant models of capitalism, "shaping a mindset that puts society's needs first".[24] An off-shoot of the Bank is the Grameen Creative Lab (GCL), a social business itself that aims to support other enterprises in their growth and development, in partnership with the enterprise software and related services company SAP AG and the Inter-American Investment Corporation (IIC). The Creative Lab's approach has three pillars. Firstly, it raises awareness of the potential of people to set up successful purpose-led profit-making enterprises, through public events, the publication of books and articles, and speaking engagements "to cultivate a constant exchange". In 2013, Grameen Creative Lab was a partner for the first EuroAsia Social Business Forum in Istanbul, an event due to take place every two years, nurturing a cross-continental culture of social enterprise, as well as supporting new markets in Turkey itself. The second pillar is to develop the public's understanding of business and its purpose, through creative workshops, experimentation with small-scale pilot businesses, and the support of academic research. The third pillar is impact: Grameen is exploring how to set up global joint ventures in social business. It also aims to create a certification methodology to enable the general public and potential investors to recognize social businesses. A certification scheme (along the lines of Fairtrade) would enhance the profile of both Grameen and any certified brands, and help to develop a common understanding of the specific characteristics that set them apart from other profit-making companies.

In Haiti, Grameen Creative Lab has initiated a local social enterprise incubator to accelerate sustainable recovery following the devastating earthquake of 12 January 2010, without dependence on foreign aid. YY Haiti Social Business Fund offers entrepreneurs support to get their idea off the ground. It begins with Grameen's seven principles of social business (developed by Yunus at the World Economic Forum in Davos in January 2009, and beginning with the objective to overcome poverty and other problems which threaten people and society – not to maximize profit), and then guides them through a series of tasks: decide which social need you want to address (e.g. malnutrition, poor education, environment); clarify your personal skills and capabilities; think about potential partners who could support you to get your project started; brainstorm your social business idea; and, finally, write an overview describing various potential solutions. Next, it explains, the entrepreneurs should discuss their business proposition with friends and business partners and try to spot any weak spots in the commercial case, before sending YY Haiti a two-page executive summary explaining the idea, the target market and the social purpose it intends to address. YY Haiti and the Grameen Creative Lab then assess the concept paper; if it qualifies as a social business, the entrepreneur is asked to write a more detailed plan.

One successful application to the YY Haiti Social Business Fund came from a group of fishermen looking to invest in better boats and equipment to enable them to reach territories further from the shore, thus bringing back more attractive stock to rival cheap imports; they also wanted to buy refrigeration facilities to extend their window for sales. A loan of $50,000, repayable over eight years, will enable them to move from subsistence fishing to this commercial model. Grameen Creative Lab notes the potential of the investment to sustain the fishers' families and communities, and to encourage the younger generation to remain by the coast in Bayeux, rather than moving to cities to seek work. It also notes that this is a shared vision, and one that could strengthen existing bonds within the community: "The fishermen have known each other for many years and have established strong relationships built on trust and friendship."

Another $110,000 investment by YY Haiti, also repayable over eight years, will boost the country's dairy industry. The milk processing company Lèt Agogo ("Milk on the go") aims to strengthen the demand for local dairy products – again, reducing Haiti's dependence on foreign imports – and to offer new opportunities to women, who are responsible for the production and bottling of the milk.

2   Fifteen

Wood-fired whole mackerel, caught by James Eaton in Cape Cornwall, I'm told on enquiring, crisped to perfection on the outside for that lovely chargrilled taste; meaty and succulent within. An accompanying punchy salsa with capers and crunchy bread bits collaborating to create quite possibly the loveliest mackerel I've eaten and laid my eyes on.

So Gabrielle Sander describes her dinner at Fifteen Cornwall in *The Arbuturian*, a magazine for "the foodie, the explorer, the stylish, the culturist, the idler". It describes its content and readers as "Unreasonably gluttonous. Inexplicably fashionable." It's not a publication that dedicates much space to social concerns. Nonetheless, Sander finds her enjoyment that evening heightened "by the knowledge that one's gluttony is for the benefit of the people" and, in light of this, "pushing the boat out to order pud, even though two more-than-adequately portioned courses have already been scraped clean, feels almost angelic. Another bottle of Shiraz? Why the hell not. It's for charity!"[25]

Fifteen Cornwall is a non-profit restaurant established to help young people from disadvantaged and difficult situations find not just work but a career in an industry they are passionate about. It was inspired by (and is a franchise of) the TV chef Jamie Oliver's first restaurant of the same name, which opened in London in 2002. Oliver was struck by the idea of cooking as a "potential career path for young unemployed people – specifically those who had fallen out of mainstream education and were in need of a fresh new start in life". By offering apprenticeships to fifteen young people a year, and helping them to find a job subsequent to their training, he hoped to match their passion for food with a purpose.

The question begs: can a sense of social purpose really enhance a meal, as Sander seems to claim? I am willing to believe it can. The way in which people relate to their food, particular in places where abundance is the problem, can be fraught with anxiety. Part of the issue is that people are disconnected from their food: few watch it grow or see it harvested, and even fewer grow or catch it themselves. Many don't cook, distancing them even further from the products on their plate. The result is disengagement from its value – the time and effort that has gone into preparing it – and from the value it brings to their health. By connecting a meal with a social cause, Fifteen doesn't simply ease the guilt associated with over-eating: it also brings people closer to a sense of the food system as a whole, and its importance to lives beyond their own. This is what Sander is getting at: she goes on to describe the "heart-warming circle", in which your bill feeds the future of young people, as well as your own appetite.

Fifteen Cornwall, which is owned by the Cornwall Foundation of Promise, doesn't serve meals weighted with worthiness, though: it has been nominated for the best fine dining experience in Cornwall.[26] The website entices the diner to visit the restaurant by promising "bold, bright flavours [sic]" and a "spectacular" view of the coast. A new painting by local artist (and surfer) Ben Allen frames the window into the kitchen with a hint of sea spray. Without depending on its social purpose to entice clients, the restaurant is nonetheless able to win their hearts through the stories of transformation it can spin. Its mission is to create the right environment to bring their potential to the surface – through "teamwork, self-discipline, hard work, learning and, perhaps most importantly, passion".

It offers a 16-month apprenticeship to around 20 young people aged 16–24 each year, including a professional qualification (NVQ Level 2) and one-to-one training. They are also schooled in sourcing produce locally and sustainably, and trained in key skills such as butchery, bakery and fish filleting – learning to see beyond the kitchen to their role as part of a much wider food system. It's the big picture that ignites both their passion for their role and their sense of purpose: "Skills are only half the ingredients", the Chief Executive Matthew Thomson remarks. "The real light-bulb moment comes when the apprentices appreciate for themselves the love and dedication that goes into the food they're cooking with. We expose them to this right from the beginning, whether it's [through] sourcing trips to producers or a chat with a supplier over the kitchen counter."

Laura Dunne, a 25-year-old from Boscastle, describes the impact on her prospects and ambitions in the 2013 Graduation Year Book: "I now look forward to going to work and I am proud of what I do … I now not only have a sound profession that I love and am passionate about, but personally I have changed too … I have learned that you don't have to shout and get angry in order to achieve your goals." After graduating from the apprenticeship, Dunne is hoping to land a job at a top restaurant. She's not put off by the knowledge that it will be hard work: "the harder you work the more you are rewarded", she says, adding that she'd like to run her own restaurant one day.

Ryan Smith, an 18-year-old from Perranporth, who admits he spent his time at school "terrorizing" his teachers, observes that his experience at Fifteen has given him something to focus on, and also "the drive to leave my past in the past". He notes the difference it has made to his self-belief: "I've learned I can be mature at times and I can succeed despite what some people might say. I have experienced how hard working in a kitchen can be but also how enjoyable it can be." Smith also reveals that his attitudes towards the people around him have shifted – both those in positions of authority and his peers: "I've also liked being part of a team, I have tried to help others through on days when they've felt down." On graduating, Smith has started working at Barbecoa, a trendy London restaurant that spotted his talent and whose praise made him feel "really proud".

Just one year after the first Fifteen opened in London, Oliver was awarded an MBE by the Queen for his work to enhance the prospects of young people. The restaurant was an immediate success, and the first franchise was set up in Amsterdam just two years down the line. This early success was boosted by a TV show following the progress of the apprentices. However, it is clear that Fifteen Cornwall is not resting on the laurels of either the show or the TV personality, who, in 2012, topped the UK Christmas book charts for the third year running.[27]

3 Nobel Prize

In this chapter, I have already mentioned two winners of the Nobel Peace Prize: Amartya Sen and Muhammad Yunus. Established by Alfred Nobel, a scientist, inventor and the founder-director of a multinational company, the Nobel Prize is arguably the most widely recognized and highly esteemed symbol of purpose. Crucially, according to the terms of Nobel's will, it rewards people who pursue knowledge and creativity, and not simply for the sake of achievement or to set a record; the prize recognizes those who "during the previous year, shall have conferred the greatest benefit to mankind". Alfred Nobel's own concern with the meaning of life led him in two directions: one was towards depression and melancholy, and the other towards research, invention and entrepreneurial energy. He made the fortune upon which the prize was established (and continues to be paid, drawing on its annual interest) through the commercial development of just a few of his 355 patents: the invention of explosives, detonators and dynamite. He ran 16 dynamite factories in 14 countries, and mostly single-handedly, keeping it together with letters and personal visits: he didn't like to delegate.[28]

Nobel was sadly misled in his declared hope that dynamite might bring an end to war, prompting all civilized nations to "retreat and disband their troops". But he was also aware that the greatest legacy he could leave would not be something of his own invention, but a means of encouraging others to lead purposeful lives. Svante Lindqvist, author or *A Tribute to the Memory of Alfred Nobel: Inventor, Entrepreneur and Insustrialist*, asks whether, were it not for the prize, Nobel would have perhaps been even better known today as a technical and industrial innovator; perhaps, but his own fame was far from his aim. He once wrote: "It appears pathetic to wish to be anyone or anything in the motley collection of 1400 million two-legged tailless apes which are running around on our orbiting terrestrial projectile." Such a seemingly misanthropic stance does not run counter to his sense of purpose. It was of little consequence to him to "be anyone of note": *doing* something of note was life's redeeming possibility. He referred to a sense of duty as "that distorted quality" – but one that would cause him to "toil until you drop". He frequently wrote of his wish to leave business life and devote himself to science: "If I have 300 ideas in a year and just one turns out to work I am satisfied".[29] Lindqvist concludes, "The true meaning of Alfred Nobel's will was perhaps this: it was intended to emphasize the importance of creative work as the only activity capable of giving real happiness and dispelling the existential fears".[30]

The Prize is now administered by the Nobel Foundation Rights Association, set up in 1999 to provide high-quality information to a growing global audience, by engaging with media, through research and through educational activities. Under this umbrella sit other arms of the brand: Nobel Media AB, which aims to spread knowledge and inspiration about the Nobel Prize-awarded achievements; the Nobel Museum, established to generate discussion around the natural sciences and culture through creative learning and exhibitions in an elegantly designed high-tech space; the Nobel Peace Center, which presents the Peace Prize laureates and their work, through multimedia and interactive technology, debates, cultural events and conferences; the Nobel Prize Education Fund, which supports educational outreach activities; and Nobel Symposia, which runs prestigious annual conferences. These events explore breakthrough areas of science and topics of particular cultural or social significance, from arms control and global HIV therapeutics and vaccines, to self-organization in society and molecular mechanisms in biological systems.

The popular prestige that this brand has in the fields of scientific research, creativity and the pursuit of peace is evident in the aspiration of other high-profile brands to be associated with it. In 2013, Christian Dior credited a Nobel Prize-winning discovery in the development of the formula behind its One Essential skincare range. According to Daila Strum, a professor at the Fashion Institute of Technology, New York, Dior "focuses strongly on connecting with the lifestyle of their customer base through a strong educational component", and so such an association is a real feather in its hat.[31]

The strength of the Nobel brand is also evident in the resilience of its reputation to controversy over certain awards – including some mistakes, in which scientists were awarded prizes for discoveries that turned out later to be mistaken or of no benefit to humanity at all.[32] This resilience is no doubt due in part to the unquestionable merit of the work of many of its recipients, beginning with the very first laureate in the field of physics, Konrad Wilhelm Rontgen for his discovery of X-rays, and including Marie Curie (who was awarded the Prize on two separate occasions), Albert Einstein, Martin Luther King and Nelson Mandela.

Others fall short of this very high bar. In 2012, the committee incited the criticism of the Chinese dissident artist Ai Weiwei, who called the award to the writer Mo Yan "an insult to humanity". His anger was motivated by the contrast of Mo's work, which he criticizes for a lack of political engagement, to the "previous quality of literature in the award". But Ai's criticism didn't detract from the commercial weight of winning an award: Mo Yan – whose name means "Don't say" – also owns a vodka brand called Mo Yan Zui, or "Don't say you're drunk", the value of which apparently shot up 100,000 per cent when he won the prize, even though it isn't actually producing or selling any vodka.[33]

Two years before, the Prize had angered the Chinese Government, who referred to the committee as "clowns" for its 2010 award to Liu Xiaobo, a jailed writer, critic and human rights activist. In 2009, it had caused wide controversy for offering the prize to Barack Obama in the first year of his presidency. At the time, Gilad Atzmon, the Israeli-born British jazz saxophonist, novelist, political activist and writer, was among those who approved. He distinguished between "Obama the Brand" and "Obama the President", asserting that the Obama Brand stands for hope and humanism, and arguing that, by awarding him the prize, the Nobel committee "basically bounded" the man to his brand. Atzmon makes the case for the Nobel Prize for Peace to be seen as a preventative mechanism, inducing a commitment to peace and shaping the future decisions of prize winners, as well as rewarding the rare success stories. "The Nobel Prize committee has hopefully pulled him in", Atzmon said of Obama, prompting, "once you accept it you may have to say no to Ziocons ['Zionist Conservatives'] at home, for people with a peace medal cannot launch wars..." However, given that Obama has since ramped up drone strikes in Afghanistan and intervened in Libya, Atzmon may have changed his mind.

The influence of the Nobel Prize stretches far beyond the purpose of its winners. By recognizing and valuing what people have achieved to the benefit of humanity, it can inspire many others to work towards similar goals. The list of female prize winners, particularly in science, is often cited to encourage more women to pursue careers in research and technology. Sharon Bertsch McGrayne, author of the book Nobel Prize Women in Science, describes the hurdles women had to overcome to pursue their research: "They worked in home and basement laboratories and in attic offices. They crawled behind furniture to attend science lectures. They worked as volunteers in universities for decades without pay – in the United States as late as the 1970s." McGrayne argues that the question is not why so few women have been named Nobel Prize winners but, in light of the problems they faced, why so many?[34] It's a strong indicator of one thing that women and men desire in life: the freedom to create meaning.

Desiring change

This is a book about movement and change. Desire, I said in the preface, propels us towards places and circumstances in which we imagine life will be somehow better. It will have more of something that we value in the world: more connections within a community; more opportunities for adventure; more stimulus for our senses – or more of something that we value in ourselves: the energy and appetite we have for life, or the meaning we give to it.

This is also a book with a purpose: to guide brands in harnessing the force of desire. If brands can understand what people value, and how they would like this value to enhance their lives, they can respond in ways that are meaningful and innovative. They will help to shape a world in which both business and people thrive.

A brand can secure its role in such a future by enhancing our lives in ways that are resilient and responsive to flux. This depends on two things. The first is a business model that doesn't erode its own foundations through a careless attitude towards the natural resources and social capital on which it depends. The second is a culture in which the brand *is* the strategy, and everyone in it wakes up each day and asks afresh, "What do people really want, and what role can I play?"

Why is it important to ask these questions again and again? Because the world is changing more rapidly than ever before: new markets are emerging; innovation is changing the face of many industries, and hyper connectivity is transforming knowledge and relationships. Not to mention the impact of 400 particles of carbon dioxide per million on seasons, storms, sea levels, supply chains and the ability of many millions to find adequate food and shelter. The demands and expectations placed on brands will go on rising as the search for new ways of sustaining our lives becomes more pressing. There will be opportunities for innovators, and risks for any business that stands still. A brand that remains open to new ways of defining its role in society, and ambition for that role to be a meaningful one, will stand a better chance of keeping up.

There is one desire I haven't yet mentioned and which is perhaps the most important, in that it is a key to unlocking all the others. This is the desire for change. What does it mean "to desire change", when the world is already in such flux? Is it not enough to adapt, with a Stoic shrug of acceptance? Perhaps, but such a response won't strengthen your brand.

Desiring change means welcoming the opportunities it can bring, and harnessing them to your purpose.

This is the opposite of the predominant model of consumerism today. Instead of welcoming change, we resist it. We weigh ourselves down with more and more objects that seem somehow to offer stability, and even come with the promise of greater choice, but in reality, they make us less adaptable to change.

The Chinese artist Song Dong illustrates this poignantly in his installation "Waste not", in which he lays out the entire contents of his mother's flat: every button, bead and bag. His mother, he explains, had kept everything in response to the extreme distress and turbulence of the Cultural Revolution, which took away the shared stories that bind and strengthen communities, and millennia-old traditions of art and music that shape and celebrate the place of people in the world. China Dream offers an alternative to the next generation: instead of offering them stability in the form of vast quantities of stuff, it offers them the chance to reconnect with their cultural history, to strengthen their relationships, and to find balance in their lives.

If we can find ways to draw strength and wellbeing from the elements of our lives that we really value – from our friends and family, from the beauty and stimulus of the world around us, or from the opportunities we have to explore it and to grow – we will become more open to change around us, and be able to find new patterns of meaning within it.

When we desire change, we also become it.

In the course of my research for this book, Marc Mathieu, Senior Vice President for Marketing at Unilever, shared with me his understanding of what brands are and what they exist to do:

> My definition of brands is that they help people to deal with their fears and anxieties and answer some fundamental questions that are left unanswered by society. Brands emerged as a product to buy and an idea to buy into. When people buy, subscribe to or use something that a brand offers, they also subscribe to an idea that very often represents a tension in society. The brand comes up with a point of view and potentially helps people make sense of it all. So when you talk about community, adventure, aesthetics, vitality and purpose, it brings me back to the question, what are we aspiring to as human beings? At different moments in time we need to learn, we need to bond, we need to defend, we need to find meaning – not just to consume, not just to acquire things. We have come to a place where brands have become synonymous with consumption, where in reality brands should also be facilitating bonding, hence community; learning, hence personal development; defending things that you care about, which is culture; meaning, hence purpose.[1]

My hope for this book is that it will support brands to develop their role in our lives in meaningful ways; in doing so, they will increase our resilience so that we can embrace change and work with us in actively shaping the world we desire. If a brand can help one person respond to change, not with fear and anxiety, but with an open heart, it will have secured a foothold in the future.

Notes to the text

Introduction: A guide to desire

1. "Who's Gone Bust in Retailing 2010–2013?", Centre for Retail Research, 21 November 2013. http://www.retailresearch.org/whosegonebust.php [Accessed 24 November 2013.]
2. A. H. Maslow (1943) "A Theory of Human Motivation", Psychological Review, 50, 370–396.
3. This quotation is widely attributed to Oscar Wilde, but also to Robert Maynard Hutchins.
4. A. M. Max-Neef, A. Elizalde, M. Hopenhayn (1991) Human Scale Development, New York: Apex Press, pp. 13–19, 32–9.
5. D. Kahneman (2010) "The riddle of experience vs. memory", TED. www.ted.com/talks/daniel_kahneman_the_riddle_of_experience_vs_memory.html [Accessed 25 August 2013.]
6. J. Elliott, J. D. Rhodes (2009) "The Value of Frustration: An Interview with Adam Phillips", World Picture 3, 2.
7. T. Crompton (2010) "Common Cause: The case for working with our cultural values", WWF-UK. http://assets.wwf.org.uk/downloads/common_cause_report.pdf [Accessed 12/04/2013.]
8. T. Levitt (1983) The Marketing Imagination, New York: The Free Press, pp. 55–6.
9. J. Neff (2012) "Revlon Counts on 'Selling Hope' to Make Up for Its Small Size", AdAge, 3 September 2012. http://adage.com/article/cmo-interviews/revlon-counts-selling-hope-make-size/236961/ [Accessed 25 August 2013.]
10. P. Kotler, H. Kartajaya, I. Setiawan (2010) Marketing 3.0: From Product to Customers to the Human Spirit, New Jersey: John Wiley & Sons, p. 4.
11. "Meaningful Brands", Havas Media (2013). http://www.havasmedia.com/meaningful-brands [Accessed 25 August 2013.]
12. "Re:Thinking Consumption", BBMG, GlobeScan and SustainAbility (2013). http://www.globescan.com/component/edocman/?view=document&id=46 &Itemid=591 [Accessed 12 March 2013.]

13. "The New Consumer in the Era of Mindful Spending", *Prosumer Report*, 8, Havas Media (2010), 4. http://www.thenewconsumer.com/wp-content/uploads/2010/11/Prosumer_Report-_The_New_Consumer_lores.pdf [Accessed 26 August 2013.]

14. BBMG et al. 2013, 7.

15. T. Levitt (1983) *The Marketing Imagination*, New York: The Free Press, pp. 55–6.

16. "China Dream", JUCCCE and Ogilvy China (2012). http://vimeo.com/51734216/ [Accessed 26 August 2013.]

17. China Dream, JUCCCE. http://www.juccce.org/chinadream.

18. A. Sedghi "Which cities do the world's millionaires and billionaires live in?", *Guardian*, 8 May 2013. http://www.guardian.co.uk/news/datablog/2013/may/08/cities-top-millionaires-billionaires [Accessed 25 August 2013.]

19. M. Fackler "Japan Power Company Admits Failings on Plant Precautions", *New York Times*, 12 October 2012. http://www.nytimes.com/2012/10/13/world/asia/tepco-admits-failure-in-acknowledging-risks-at-nuclear-plant.html?_r=1& [Accessed 26 August 2013.]

20. Exclusive interview with the author, London, 9 April 2013. See also: www.shadow-candle.com [Accessed 26 August 2013.]

21. A. Marks "The Relative size of things and our changing roles", *PageTurner Blog*, 12 March 2013. http://www.awpagesociety.com/2013/03/the-relative-size-of-things/ [Accessed 10 July 2013.]

22. M. McLuhan (1994) *Understanding Media: The Extensions of Man*, 2nd edn, Cambridge, MA: MIT Press, pp. 8–12.

23. J.-B. Danet, N. Liddell, L. Dobney, D. MacKenzie, T. Allen (2013) *Business is Beautiful: The hard art of standing apart*, London: LID Publishing, pp. 8–9.

24. "The State of Marketing, IBM's Global Survey of Marketers", IBM (2013). http://public.dhe.ibm.com/common/ssi/ecm/en/zzj12347usen/ZZJ12347USEN.PDF [Accessed 26 August 2013.]

25. "The State of Social Consumer Service", NM Incite (2012), 1.

Chapter 1   Community

1. "Ice Age art: arrival of the modern mind", British Museum (2013). www.britishmuseum.org/whats_on/past_exhibitions/2013/ice_age_art/about_the_exhibition.aspx [Accessed 26 August 2013.]

2. R. Girard (1961) *Mensonge romantique et vérité romanesque*, Paris: Grasset.

3. S. Townsend (2013) "The Naked Environmentalist", Futerra, 4. www.futerra.co.uk/wp-content/uploads/2013/05/The-Naked-Environmentalist.pdf [Accessed 26 August 2013.]

4. Exclusive interview with the author, London and Madrid, 21 March 2013.

5. S. Adballah, J. Michaelson, S. Shah, L. Stoll, N. Marks (2012) "Happy Planet Index: 2012 Report", new economics foundation. Available from: www.neweconomics.org/publications/entry/happy-planet-index-2012-report [Accessed 26 August 2013.]

6. A. Simpson "Back to basics with social theory", *Green Futures*, 17 February 2012. www.forumforthefuture.org/greenfutures/articles/back-basics-with-social-theory [Accessed 26 August 2013.]

7. R. Sennett (2012) *Together: The Rituals, Pleasures and Politics of Cooperation*, London, Penguin, pp. ix–x, 94–5.

8. Simpson 2012.

9. J. Helliwell, C. Barrington-Leigh, A. Harris and H. Huang (2009) "International Evidence on the Social Context of Wellbeing", NBER Working Paper Series, 14720. Available from: www.nber.org/papers/w14720 [Accessed 26 August 2013]; "A Sense of Belonging: A joint strategy for improving the mental health and wellbeing of Lothian's population 2011–2016", NHS Lothian (2011). www.nhslothian.scot.nhs.uk/OurOrganisation/Strategies/Documents/SenseOfBelonging.pdf [Accessed 26 August 2013.]

10. N. Lowery "The importance of community in business", *North Idaho Business Journal*, 26 March 2013. http://nibusinessjournal.com/2013/03/the-importance-of-community-in-business/ [Accessed 17 July 2013.]

11. "Smarter Cities Challenge: Málaga, Spain", IBM Smarter Cities Challenge, 15 August 2012. http://www.youtube.com/watch?v=aWPt-bpPjSQ&feature=share&list=UULpSQ6MgG1TDYzvbbcT8USg

12. J. Lacan (2001) "The Mirror Stage as Formative of the Function of the I as Revealed in Psychoanalytic Experience", *The Norton Anthology of Theory and Criticism*, Vincent B. Leitch et al. (eds), New York: W. W. Norton & Company, 1285–90.

13. Exclusive interview with the author, 6 June 2013.

14. J.-J. Rousseau (2012) *The Social Contract*, South Australia, University of Adelaide.

15. D. E. Wittkower (ed.) (2010) *Facebook and Philosophy: What's on your mind?*, Chicago and La Salle, Illinois: Open Court, p. 98.

16. K. Harrison, J. Cantor (1997) "The relationship between media consumption and eating disorders", *Journal of Communication* 47: 1, 40–67; J. L. Derenne, E. V. Beresin (2006) "Body Image, Media, and Eating Disorders", *Academic Psychiatry* 30:3, 257–61.

17. Exclusive interview with the author, London, 2 April 2013.

18. J. Elliott, J. D. Rhodes (2009) "The Value of Frustration: An Interview with Adam Phillips", World Picture 3, 7.

19. A. Phillips, B. Taylor (2013) *On Kindness*, London: Penguin, p. 17.

20. Ibid, p. 21.

21. Exclusive interview with the author, Hastings, 29 July 2013.

22. R. A. Howell (2012) "It's not (just) 'the environment, stupid!' Values, motivations, and routes to engagement of people adopting lower-carbon lifestyles", *Global Environmental Change*, 23:1, 10. Available from: http://dx.doi.org/10.1016/j.gloenvcha.2012.10.015 [Accessed 26 August 2013.]

23. L. Chawla (1995) "Life Paths into Effective Environmental Action", *Journal of Environmental Education*, 31, 15–26; J. Wolf "Ecological Citizenship as Public

Engagement with Climate Change" in Whitmarsh, L., O'Neill, S., Lorenzoni, I. (eds) (2011) *Engaging the Public with Climate Change: Behaviour Change and Communication*, London: Earthscan pp. 120–37; R. Osbaldiston, K. M. Sheldon (2003) "Promoting internalized motivation for environmentally responsible behavior: A prospective study of environmental goals", *Journal of Environmental Psychology* 23, 349–57.

24. V. Grinnell-Wright, "Does 5% make Justgiving a digital friend or foe for charity", *Charity Mash*, 2 June 2009. http://charitymash.com/2009/does-5-make-justgiving-a-digital-friend-or-foe-for-charity/ [Accessed 26 August 2013.]; R. Cellan-Jones "Believe.in and the business of charity", *BBC News Technology*, 22 April 2013. http://www.bbc.co.uk/news/technology-22245601 [Accessed 26 August 2013.]

25. V. Marsh "Social impact bonds help charity tackle homelessness", *Green Futures*, 1 July 2013. http://www.forumforthefuture.org/greenfutures/articles/social-impact-bonds-help-charity-tackle-homelessness [Accessed 26 August 2013.]

26. J. Novogratz (2011) "Inspiring a life of immersion", TED. http://www.ted.com/talks/jacqueline_novogratz_inspiring_a_life_of_immersion.html [Accessed 26 August 2013.]

27. "Over 1.7m katchi abadi dwellers given property rights", *Daily Times*, 13 March 2013. http://www.dailytimes.com.pk/default.asp?page=2013%5C03%5C13%5Cstory_13-3-2013_pg13_1 [Accessed 13 July 2013.]

28. www.amcpakistan.org [Accessed 26 August 2013.]

29. "Noorghazi Impact Study August 2010 to January 2013", The Pakpur Foundation (2013). http://www.pakpur.org/Noorghaz%20Impact%20Study%20Aug%202010%20-%20Jan%202013.pdf [Accessed 26 August 2013.]

30. Exclusive interview with the author, Skype, 29 July 2013.

31. "Made in Lower East Side Detailed Overview", miLES (2012). http://issuu.com/madeinles/docs/overview [Accessed 26 August 2013.]

32. miLES Introduction, 12 June 2013. http://www.youtube.com/watch?v=MZVu3mzg5Zs [Accessed 26 August 2013.]

33. http://www.madeinles.org/about/ [Accessed 26 August 2013.]

34. miLES 2013.

35. "Stefan Orlowski on Responsible Leadership", *Business in the Community News & Events*, 9 January 2012. http://www.bitc.org.uk/blog/post/stefan-orlowski-responsible-leadership#sthash.IRnYZo3r.dpuf [Accessed 29 July 2013.]

36. Use Your Local. http://www.useyourlocal.com/manifesto/pubs/starpubs/ [Accessed 26 August 2013.]

37. "Star Pubs & Bars (part of the HEINEKEN Company) lessee support package", *Business in the Community Case Studies*, July 2013. http://www.bitc.org.uk/our-resources/case-studies/star-pubs-bars-part-heineken-company-lessee-support-package#sthash.tTcgtA6F.pCb0PoBj.dpuf [Accessed 26 August 2013.]

38. Ibid.
39. M. Taylor "Eating out in Bristol – Mark Taylor reviews Eastfield Inn, Henleaze Road", *Bristol Post*, 26 July 2013. http://www.bristolpost.co.uk/Eating-Bristol-Mark-Taylor-reviews-Eastfield-Inn/story-19574728-detail/story.html [Accessed 26 August 2013.]
40. http://www.henleazeoldboys.co.uk/player%20profiles/profile_anderson. html [Accessed 26 August 2013.]

Chapter 2   Adventure

1. R. Girard (1961) *Mensonge romantique et vérité Romanesque*, Paris: Grasset.
2. E. W. Said (1994) *Culture and Imperialism*, London: Vintage, p. xiii.
3. Ibid, p. 80
4. R. Prime (1997) *Ramayana: A Journey*, London: Collins and Brown, pp. 6–7.
5. H. Giroux "How Disney Magic and the Corporate Media Shape Youth Identity in the Digital Age", *Truthout*, 21 August 2011. http://www.truth-out.org/opinion/item/2808:how-disney-magic-and-the-corporate-media-shape-youth-identity-in-the-digital-age [Accessed 26 August 2013.]
6. Ibid.
7. B. Barnes "Disney Expert Uses Science to Draw Boy Viewers", *New York Times*, 13 April 2009. http://www.nytimes.com/2009/04/14/arts/television/14boys.html?pagewanted=all&_r=0 [Accessed 26 August 2013.]
8. "Global Trends 2030: Alternative Worlds", National Intelligence Council (2012). http://www.dni.gov/files/documents/GlobalTrends_2030.pdf [Accessed 26 August 2013.]
9. http://www.erbucky.com/ [Accessed 24 November 2013.]
10. G. Wolf "The Data-Driven Life", *New York Times*, 28 April 2010. http://www.nytimes.com/2010/05/02/magazine/02self-measurement-t.html?pagewanted=all [Accessed 20 December 2013.]
11. C. Hollindale "Nike+ FuelBand and Google Glass: what next for the 'quantified self'?", *Guardian*, 27 March 2013. http://www.theguardian.com/technology/2013/mar/27/nike-fuelband-google-glass-quantified-self [Accessed 20 December 2013.]
12. D. Else "road.cc test report", 16 January 2013. http://road.cc/content/review/73674-mule-bar-kicks-energy-gel-box-24 [Accessed 26 August 2013.]

Chapter 3   Aesthetics

1. A. R. Humphreys (ed.) (1981) *Much Ado About Nothing*, Act II iii, l.230, London: The Arden Shakespeare, p. 141.
2. T. Jackson (2009) *Prosperity Without Growth,* London: Earthscan, p. 40.
3. V. Postrel (2004) *The Substance of Style: How the rise of aesthetic value is remaking commerce, culture and consciousness*, New York: Perennial, Harper-Collins Publishers, p. xi.

4. A. de Botton (2006), *The Architecture of Happiness: The secret art of furnishing your life*, London: Penguin, p. 11.
5. P. Miles "Artists bring beauty to emergency housing", *Green Futures*, 17 May 2013. http://www.forumforthefuture.org/greenfutures/articles/artists-bring-beauty-emergency-housing [Accessed 26 August 2013.]
6. D. Blackburn "Interview with a writer: Evgeny Morozov", *The Spectator*, 26 April 2013. http://blogs.spectator.co.uk/books/2013/04/interview-with-a-writer-evgeny-morozov/ [Accessed 26 August 2013.]
7. T. Masters "Punchdrunk's *The Drowned Man* is theatre on a grand scale", *BBC News*, 19 July 2013. http://bbc.co.uk/news/entertainment-arts-23329899 [Accessed 26 August 2013.]
8. "Consumers in 2030, Forecasts and Projections for Life in 2030", Forum for the Future and Which? (2013) 8. http://www.forumforthefuture.org/sites/default/files/project/downloads/future2030-finalreport.pdf [Accessed 26 August 2013.]
9. E. Carter trans., Epictetus, *The Enchiridion*, The Internet Classics Archive. http://classics.mit.edu/Epictetus/epicench.html#74 [Accessed 26 August 2013.]
10. H. Jenkins (ed.) (1982) *Hamlet*, Act II ii, l.250, London: The Arden Shakespeare, p. 250.
11. J. Confino "Patagonia plans global campaign for responsible capitalism", *Guardian*, 11 February 2013. http://www.theguardian.com/sustainable-business/blog/patagonia-campaign-responsible-capitalism [Accessed 26 August 2013.]
12. Exclusive interview with the author, London, 9 May 2013.
13. R. Hine, C. Wood, J. Barton, J. Pretty (2011) "The mental health and wellbeing effects of a walking and outdoor activity based therapy project", Discovery Quest and Julian Housing; R. Hine, J. Peacock, J. Pretty (2008) "Care farming in the UK: Contexts, benefits and links with therapeutic communities", *International Journal of Therapeutic Communities* 29:3.
14. F. A. Bernstein "A house not for mere mortals", *New York Times*, 3 April 2008. http://www.nytimes.com/2008/04/03/garden/03destiny.html?pagewanted=all&_r=0 [Accessed 26 August 2013.]
15. G. Bachelard (1994), *The Poetics of Space*, Boston: Beacon Press, pp. 33–4.
16. V. Woolf (1992) *To the Lighthouse*, London: Penguin, pp. 144–5.
17. http://newsroom.cisco.com/feature-content?type=webcontent&articleId=1208342 and http://share.cisco.com/internet-of-things.html [Accessed 26 August 2013.]
18. K. Ashton "That 'Internet of Things' Thing", *RFID Journal*, 22 June 2009. http://www.rfidjournal.com/articles/view?4986 [Accessed 26 August 2013.]
19. M. Chui, M. Löffler, and R. Roberts "The Internet of Things", *McKinsey Quarterly*, March 2010. http://www.mckinsey.com/insights/high_tech_telecoms_internet/the_internet_of_things [Accessed 26 August 2013.]

20. "Internet of Things in 2020: A Roadmap for the future", Infso D.4 Networked Enterprise and RFID Infso G.2 Micro & Nanosystems in co-operation with the RFID Working Group of the European Technology Platform on Smart Systems Integration (2008). ftp://ftp.cordis.europa.eu/pub/fp7/ict/docs/enet/internet-of-things-in-2020-ec-eposs-workshop-report-2008-v3_en.pdf [Accessed 26 August 2013.]

21. http://new-aesthetic.tumblr.com/ and http://www.evan-roth.com/work/multi-touch-finger-paintings/ [Accessed 26 August 2013.]

22. www.ikeahackers.net [Accessed 26 August 2013.]

23. http://www.forumforthefuture.org/project/wired-change/more/our-hackathons [Accessed 26 August 2013.]

24. http://www.mauimakers.com/blog/about/ [Accessed 26 August 2013.]

25. http://www.dyvikdesign.com/site/research/fablab/fabcafe-in-tokyo.html [Accessed 26 August 2013.]

26. K. Swisher "MakerBot Sells to Stratasys for $403M — Plus $201M for Earn-Outs — as 3-D Printing Market Explodes", *All Things D*, 19 June 2013. http://allthingsd.com/20130619/makerbot-sells-to-stratasys-for-403m-plus-201m-for-earn-outs-as-3-d-printing-market-explodes/ [Accessed 26 August 2013.]

27. BBMG et al. 2013, 6.

28. Exclusive interview with the author, London, 16 March 2013.

29. India's handicraft exports rise 13% on US demand, *Fibre2Fasion*, 21 May 2013. http://www.fibre2fashion.com/news/textile-news/newsdetails.aspx?news_id=146354 [Accessed 26 August 2013.]

30. "Bali's bamboo craft exports up by 22.8 per cent", *The Jakarta Post*, 5 March 2013. http://www.thejakartapost.com/bali-daily/2013-03-05/bali-s-bamboo-craft-exports-228-percent.html [Accessed 26 August 2013.]

31. A. Simpson "Is luxury the new epitome of green values?", *Green Futures*, 29 March 2012. http://www.forumforthefuture.org/greenfutures/articles/luxury-new-epitome-green-values [Accessed 26 August 2013.]

32. Exclusive interview with the author, London, 23 April 2013.

33. Exclusive interview with the author, Hastings, 10 August 2013; "Design Industry in India, Gunjan Gupta", British Council Arts, http://vimeo.com/21160160 [Accessed 26 August 2013.]; http://creativeconomy.britishcouncil.org/people/gunjan-gupta/ [Accessed 26 August 2013.]

34. S. S. Barlingay (2006) *A modern introduction to Indian aesthetic theory*, New Delhi: D. K. Printworld.

35. V. Ganapati Sthapati, former Principal of the Government College of Architecture and Sculpture, Mahabalipuram. http://www.vastuved.com/profile.html [Accessed 26 August 2013.]

36. Niranjan Babu, Chief Editor, The Astrological eMagazine. http://www.astrologicalmagazine.com/ http://www.niranjanbabu.com/generaltips.html [Accessed 26 August 2013.]

37. http://www.wrap.co.in/spaces/spaces3.html [Accessed 26 August 2013.]
38. S. S. Chowdhury "Global designer Gunjan Gupta creates sculptural and cultural furniture", *India Today*, 15 May 2012. http://indiatoday.intoday.in/story/gunjan-gupta-sculptural-cultural-furniture-indigenous-crafts/1/188844.html [Accessed 26 August 2013.]
39. P. Dazeley, C. Houston-Price (2012) "Exposure to food's non-taste sensory properties: A nursery intervention to increase children's willingness to eat fruit and vegetables", School of Psychology & Clinical Language Sciences, University of Reading. Available from: http://www.ellaskitchen.co.uk/wp-content/uploads/2012/03/The-grown-up-research.pdf [Accessed 6 August 2013.]

Chapter 4   Vitality

1. http://www.nytimes.com/1996/07/20/style/20iht-pic.t.html; http://en.wiki pedia.org/wiki/Ch%C3%A2teau_Grimaldi_(Antibes)
2. R. M. Ryan, C. Frederick (1997) "On Energy, Personality and Health: Subjective vitality as a dynamic reflection of wellbeing", *Journal of Personality* 65:3, 529–65; 530.
3. Ibid.
4. A. Ginsberg "'March: Demonstration as spectacle, as example, as communication" in A. Charles (ed.) (2002) *The Portable Sixties Reader*, London: Penguin, pp. 208–12.
5. The movement now calls itself LGBT Pride, recognizing lesbian, bisexual and transgender rights too.
6. P. Petit (2012) "The Journey Across the High Wire", TED. http://www.ted.com/talks/philippe_petit_the_journey_across_the_high_wire.html [Accessed 26 August 2013.]
7. H. Jenkins "What Samba Schools Can Teach Us About Participatory Culture", 14 November 2011. http://henryjenkins.org/2011/11/what_samba_schools_can_teach_u.html [Accessed 26 August 2013.]
8. http://www.la2050.org/indicators/arts-cultural-vitality/ and http://www.la2050.org/site/assets/files/1454/la2050_report_021913.pdf [Accessed 08 August 2013.]
9. World Cities Culture Report, Mayor of London (2012). http://www.london.gov.uk/sites/default/files/archives/lcsg-docs-WorldCitiesCultureReport.pdf [Accessed 26 August 2013.]
10. R. Bruner "Is medicine on the wrong track?" *Toledo Blade*, 30 April 1961, 2: 1. http://news.google.com/newspapers?nid=1350&dat=19610430&id=WqF OAAAAIBAJ&sjid=DwEEAAAAIBAJ&pg=7088,4521367 [Accessed 8 August 2013.]
11. "Five Ways to Wellbeing", new economics foundation, NHS Confederation (2011). Available from: http://www.neweconomics.org/publications/entry/five-ways-to-wellbeing [Accessed 8 August 2013.]

12. http://www.unilever.co.uk/aboutus/introductiontounilever/vitality/Default.aspx [Accessed 26 August 2013.]
13. Unilever is working towards this goal through the brand campaign Unilever Project Sunlight: http://www.unilever.co.uk/brands-in-action/detail/Project-sunlight/377328/ [Accessed 13 December 2013.]
14. http://www.intrinsi.ca/who-we-are/why-choose-osteopathic-therapy [Accessed 26 August 2013.]
15. Exclusive interview with the author, 20 August 2013.
16. http://www.sunsilk.in/styletrends/Highlight-your-hair-and-your-personality.aspx [Accessed 26 August 2013.]
17. Exclusive interview with the author, 1 June 2013.
18. The Air Pollution Index measures concentrations of ambient respiratory suspended particulate (RSP), sulphur dioxide (SO_2), carbon monoxide (CO), ozone (O_3) and nitrogen dioxide (NO_2) over a 24-hour period, and rates them according to the potential health effects.
19. A. Kuczynski "Just Dance", *Harper's Bazaar*, 8 March 2013. http://www.harpersbazaar.com/beauty/health-wellness-articles/benefits-of-zumba-class-0313#slide-1 [Accessed 26 August 2013.]
20. Video at http://www.zumba.com/en-US/about# [Accessed 9 August 2013.]
21. http://www.zumba.org.uk/page5.html [Accessed 9 August 2013.]
22. http://www.rd.com/advice/work-career/meet-the-man-behind-zumba-beto-perez/ [Accessed 09 August 2013.]
23. L. Kwoh "Zumba CEO: Every Time You Let Someone Go, 'It's a Scar'", *The Wall Street Journal*, 20 March 2013. http://blogs.wsj.com/atwork/2013/03/20/zumba-ceo-every-time-you-let-someone-go-its-a-scar/ [Accessed 9 August 2013.]
24. http://www.lorettaclaiborne.com/ [Accessed 9 August 2013.]
25. D. Pomerantz "The Celebrity 100: How We Create The List", *Forbes*, 26 June 2013. http://www.forbes.com/sites/dorothypomerantz/2013/06/26/the-celebrity-100-how-we-create-the-list/ and D. Pomerantz "Oprah Winfrey Regains No. 1 Slot On Forbes 2013 List Of The Most Powerful Celebrities". http://www.forbes.com/sites/dorothypomerantz/2013/06/26/oprah-winfrey-regains-no-1-slot-on-forbes-2013-list-of-the-most-powerful-celebrities/ [Accessed 2 August 2013.]
26. "The Ultimate O Interview: Oprah Answers All Your Questions", *O*, May 2010. http://www.oprah.com/omagazine/Oprah-Gets-Interviewed-by-O-Readers/2 [Accessed 2 August 2013.]
27. "Ellen DeGeneres Stands in Her Truth" (1997), *Oprah's Life Class*, 13 October 2011. http://www.oprah.com/oprahs-lifeclass/Ellen-DeGeneres-Stands-in-Her-Truth-Video_1 [Accessed 2 August 2013.]
28. Ibid.
29. http://www.ellentv.com/2012/10/29/madonnas-message-to-ellen/ [Accessed 2 August 2013.]

30. T. Geoghegan "Oprah Winfrey: 10 moments that made her", *BBC*, 25 May 2011. http://www.bbc.co.uk/news/world-us-canada-13507344 [Accessed 2 August 2013.]

31. "Oprah Winfrey makes 'biggest' donation to new museum", *BBC*, 12 June 2013. http://www.bbc.co.uk/news/entertainment-arts-22875375

32. http://www.oprah.com/pressroom/About-Oprahs-Angel-Network [Accessed 2 August 2013.]

Chapter 5   Purpose

1. London 2012 Facts & Figures, 27 March 2013, International Olympic Committee. http://www.olympic.org/content/olympism-in-action/olympic-legacy/london-2012-legacy/ [Accessed 26 August 2013.]

2. www.nestlecocoaplan.com [Accessed 26 August 2013.]

3. The GoodPurpose Team "The Growing Trend of Social Purpose in India", Edelman, 20 June 2012. http://purpose.edelman.com/the-growing-trend-of-social-purpose-in-india/ [Accessed 26 August 2013.]

4. A. Sen (1999) *Development as Freedom*, Oxford: Oxford University Press, p. 36.

5. Ibid, p. 37.

6. "Diarrhoea: Why children are still dying and what can be done", Unicef / WHO (2009).

7. www.unilever.com/brands-in-action/detail/Lifebuoy-creates-innovative-roti-reminder/3463 [Accessed 26 August 2013.]

8. http://www.youtube.com/helpachildreach5/ [Accessed 26 August 2013.]

9. www.lifebuoy.com/healthmap/default.aspx [Accessed 26 August 2013.]

10. "20 students fall ill after eating birthday chocolates", *Business Standard*, 14 August 2013. http://www.business-standard.com/article/pti-stories/20-students-fall-ill-after-eating-birthday-chocolates-113081400892_1.html [Accessed 26 August 2013.]

11. Hulme Hall Ringo Starr debut with The Beatles http://m.youtube.com/watch?v=yZFHL2jX1Ns&de [Accessed 26 August 2013.]

12. www.bbc.co.uk/religions/religions/christianity/subdivisions/quakers_1.shtml [Accessed 26 August 2013.]

13. R. C. Anderson, "Getting there: Ray's story" www.interfaceinc.com/getting_there/Ray.html [Accessed 26 August 2013.]

14. S. Parr "Is your business working on purpose?", *Fast Company*, 24 April 2013. http://m.fastcompany.com/3008748/your-business-working-purpose [Accessed 26 August 2013.]

15. A. McGrory-Dixon, "Purpose-driven performance management leads to organizational success", *Benefitspro*, 15 February 2013. http://m.benefitspro.com/2013/02/15/purpose-driven-performance-management-leads-to-org [Accessed 26 August 2013.]

16. "Executives and Employees Believe US Businesses Are Falling Short on Delivering Positive and Meaningful Societal Impact", *Deloitte*, 16 May 2013. http://www.deloitte.com/view/en_US/us/press/Press-Releases/2e f0c9cb719ae310VgnVCM1000003256f70aRCRD.htm [Accessed 26 August 2013.]

17. C. Conley (2011) "Getting more mojo from Maslow", *Design Mind*. http:// designmind.frogdesign.com/articles/and-now-the-good-news/getting-more-mojo-from-maslow.html [Accessed 26 August 2013.]

18. http://www.otesha.org.uk/about-us; L. McDowell "Non-hierarchical structures: could it work for you?", *Guardian*, 2 July 2012. http://www.theguardian. com/voluntary-sector-network/2012/jul/02/charities-non-hierarchical-structures [Accessed 26 August 2013.]

19. http://www.otesha.org.uk/about-us/what-we-stand-for/an-anti-oppression-manifesto and http://www.amazon.co.uk/Challenging-Oppression-Confronting-Privilege-Mullaly/dp/0195429702 [Accessed 26 August 2013.]

20. M. Abrash "Valve: How I Got Here, What It's Like, and What I'm Doing", 13 April 2012. http://blogs.valvesoftware.com/abrash/valve-how-i-got-here-what-its-like-and-what-im-doing-2/ [Accessed 26 August 2013.]

21. *Valve Handbook* (2012) Washington: Valve Press, p. 6. http://media. steampowered.com/apps/valve/Valve_Handbook_LowRes.pdf [Accessed 26 August 2013.]

22. B. Goldfarb "Voluntourism: one answer to local resource shortages", *Green Futures*, 31 January 2013. www.forumforthefuture.org/greenfutures/articles/voluntourism-one-answer-local-resource-shortages [Accessed 26 August 2013.]

23. http://www.grameencreativelab.com/a-concept-to-eradicate-poverty/7-principles.html [Accessed 26 August 2013.]

24. "Grameen Academia Report Social Business", The Grameen Creative Lab (2013). http://issuu.com/grameencl/docs/gcl_academia_report_2013_web/ 9?e=8401782/3751402 [Accessed 26 August 2013.]

25. G. Sander "Beside the Seaside: Fifteen Cornwall", *The Arbuturian*, 19 August 2013. http://www.arbuturian.com/2013/fifteen-cornwall [Accessed 26 August 2013.]

26. http://www.cornwalltoday.co.uk/awards/vote-now/ [Accessed 26 August 2013.]

27. A. Flood "Jamie Oliver tops Christmas book charts", the *Guardian*, 18 December 2012. http://www.theguardian.com/books/2012/dec/18/jamie-oliver-christmas-book-charts [Accessed 26 August 2013.]

28. S. Lindqvist (2001) *A Tribute to the Memory of Alfred Nobel: Inventor, Entrepreneur and Industrialist (1833–1896)*, trans. B. Vowles, Sweden: Royal Swedish Academy of Engineering Sciences (IVA), p. 19.

29. Ibid, pp. 36-7.

30. Ibid, p. 39.

31. J. King "Dior boasts Nobel Prize-winning ingredient in new skincare line via microsite", *Luxury Daily*, 22 August 2013. http://www.luxurydaily.com/dior-boasts-noble-prize-winning-ingredient-in-new-skincare-line-via-microsite/ [Accessed 26 August 2013.]

32. For instance, Johannes Fibiger and Julius Wagner-Jauregg for medicine. See K. Davidson "Some mistakes in Nobel history", *Chronicle Science Writer*, 8 October 2001. http://www.sfgate.com/science/article/Some-mistakes-in-Nobel-history-Even-the-judges-2870259.php [Accessed 26 August 2013.]

33. "Vodka Brand Hits Nobel Prize Jackpot", Ria Novosti, 30 October 2012. http://en.rian.ru/world/20121030/177044778.html [Accessed 26 August 2013.]

34. S. Bertsch McGrayne (2001) *Women in Science*, 2nd edn, Washington: National Academy of Sciences.

Afterword: Desiring change

1. Exclusive interview with the author, 6 June 2013.

Further Reading

Books and collections

Bachelard, G. (1994) *The Poetics of Space*, Boston: Beacon Press.

Danet, J. B. et al. (2013) *Business is Beautiful: The hard art of standing apart*, London: LID Publishing.

De Botton, A. (2006) *The Architecture of Happiness*, London: Penguin.

Jackson, T. (2009) *Prosperity Without Growth*, London: Earthscan.

Kotler, P. et al. (2012) *Marketing 3.0: From Product to Customers to the Human Spirit*, New Jersey: John Wiley & Sons.

Levitt, T. (1983) *The Marketing Imagination*, New York: The Free Press.

Maslow, A. H. (1943) "A Theory of Human Motivation", *Psychological Review*, 50.

Max-Neef, A. M. et al. (1991) *Human Scale Development*, New York: Apex Press.

McGrayne, S. Bertsch (2001) *Women in Science*, 2nd edn, Washington: National Academy of Sciences.

McLuhan, M. (1994) *Understanding Media: The Extensions of Man*, 2nd edn, Cambridge, MA: MIT Press.

Phillips, A., Taylor, B. (2013) *On Kindness*, London: Penguin.

Postrel, V. (2004) *The Substance of Style*, New York: Perennial, HarperCollins Publishers.

Said, E. W. (1994) *Culture and Imperialism*, London: Vintage.

Sen, A. (1999) *Development as Freedom*, Oxford: Oxford University Press.

Sennett, R. (2012) *Together: The Rituals, Pleasures and Politics of Cooperation*, London, Penguin.

Wittkower, D. E. (ed.) (2010) *Facebook and Philosophy: What's on your mind?*, Chicago and La Salle, Illinois: Open Court.

Reports

Adballah, S. et al. (2010) "Happy Planet Index: 2012 Report", new economics foundation. www.neweconomics.org/publications/entry/happy-planet-index-2012-report

Crompton, T. (2010) "Common Cause: The case for working with our cultural values", WWF-UK. http://assets.wwf.org.uk/downloads/common_cause_report.pdf

"Consumers in 2030, Forecasts and Projections for Life in 2030", Forum for the Future and Which? (2013). http://www.forumforthefuture.org/sites/default/files/project/downloads/future2030-finalreport.pdf

"Five Ways to Wellbeing", new economics foundation, NHS Confederation (2011). http://www.neweconomics.org/publications/entry/five-ways-to-wellbeing

"Global Trends 2030: Alternative Worlds", National Intelligence Council (2012). http://www.dni.gov/files/documents/GlobalTrends_2030.pdf

"Meaningful Brands", Havas Media (2013). http://www.havasmedia.com/meaningful-brands

"Re:Thinking Consumption", BBMG, GlobeScan and SustainAbility (2013). http://www.globescan.com/component/edocman/?view=document&id=46&Itemid=591

"The New Consumer in the Era of Mindful Spending", *Prosumer Report*, 8, Havas Media (2010). http://www.thenewconsumer.com/wp-content/uploads/2010/11/Prosumer_Report-_The_New_Consumer_lores.pdf

"The State of Marketing, IBM's Global Survey of Marketers", IBM (2013). http://public.dhe.ibm.com/common/ssi/ecm/en/zzj12347usen/ZZJ12347USEN.PDF

Townsend, S. (2013) "The Naked Environmentalist", Futerra. www.futerra.co.uk/wp-content/uploads/2013/05/The-Naked-Environmentalist.pdf

World Cities Culture Report, Mayor of London (2012). http://www.london.gov.uk/sites/default/files/archives/lcsg-docs-WorldCitiesCultureReport.pdf

Index

Brands

Concepts and keywords

Places (Cities, Countries, Continents)

People

Printed and bound by CPI Group (UK) Ltd, Croydon, CR0 4YY